I0695687

THE ART OF PERSUASION

HOW TO INFLUENCE OTHERS ETHICALLY

DAVID SANDUA

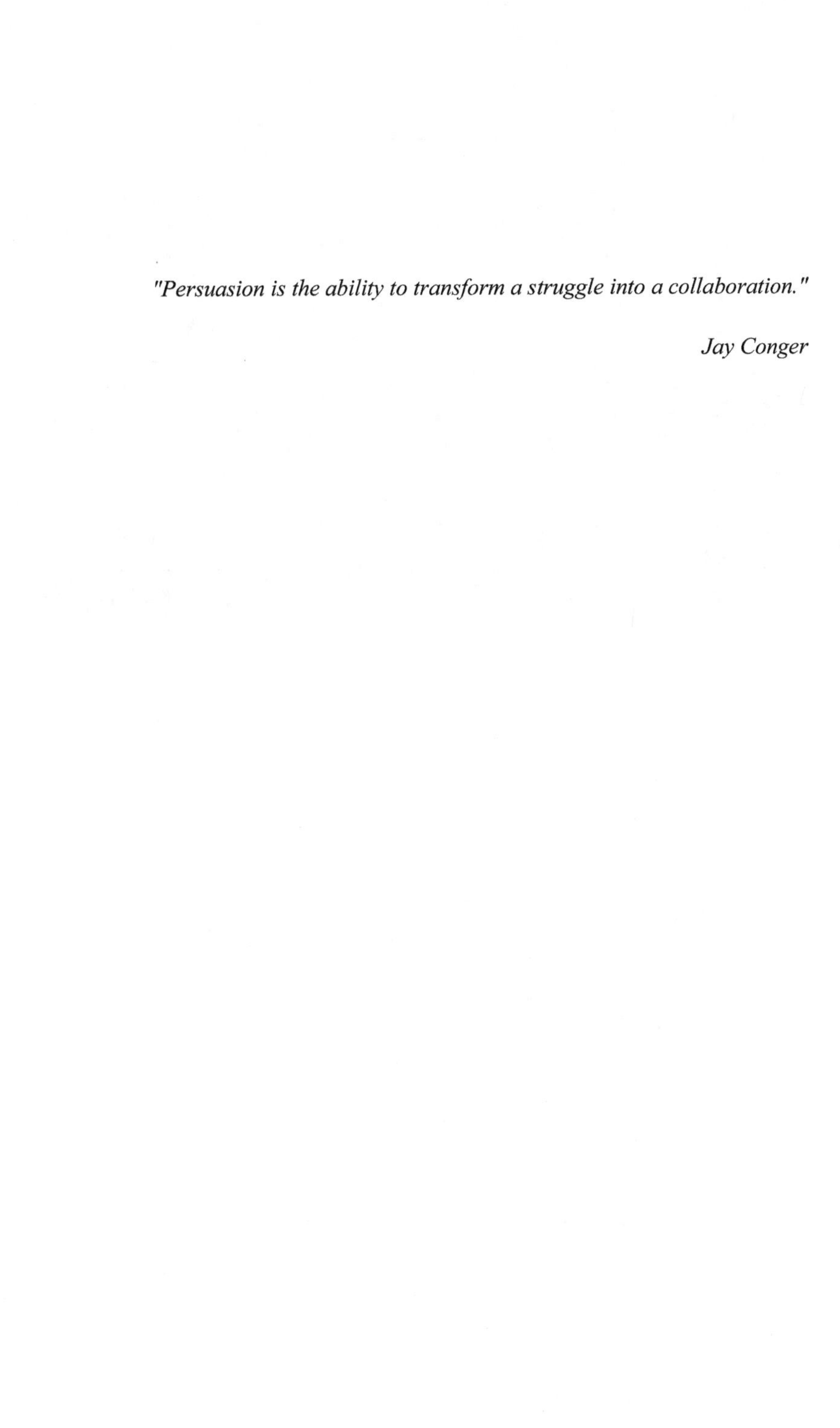

"Persuasion is the ability to transform a struggle into a collaboration."

Jay Conger

INDEX

INTRODUCTION 9

THE ART OF PERSUASION: HOW TO INFLUENCE OTHERS ETHICALLY 13

DEFINITION OF PERSUASION, ITS IMPORTANCE, AND ITS ETHICAL IMPLICATIONS.........19

I.   THE PSYCHOLOGY OF PERSUASION 27

    A.   PRINCIPLES OF PERSUASION 31

        RECIPROCITY: THE POWER OF GIVING AND RECEIVING..33

        SOCIAL PROOF: THE INFLUENCE OF OTHERS' ACTIONS ON OUR DECISION-MAKING.................37

        AUTHORITY: THE IMPACT OF PERCEIVED EXPERTISE OR AUTHORITY FIGURES..........................41

        CONSISTENCY: THE DESIRE TO ALIGN WITH OUR PAST COMMITMENTS 43

        LIKING: THE INFLUENCE OF AFFECTION AND SIMILARITY ON PERSUASION.........................47

        SCARCITY: THE ALLURE OF LIMITED RESOURCES OR OPPORTUNITIES............................49

    B.   COGNITIVE BIASES 51

        CONFIRMATION BIAS...55

        ANCHORING BIAS: THE OVERRELIANCE ON INITIAL INFORMATION 59

        AVAILABILITY BIAS: THE TENDENCY TO RELY ON READILY AVAILABLE INFORMATION WHEN MAKING JUDGMENTS 63

        LOSS AVERSION: THE GREATER WEIGHT GIVEN TO POTENTIAL LOSSES OVER EQUIVALENT GAINS...67

        FRAMING EFFECT: THE INFLUENCE OF HOW INFORMATION IS PRESENTED OR FRAMED..........69

II.   EFFECTIVE COMMUNICATION TECHNIQUES...75

    A.   ACTIVE LISTENING..79

        IMPORTANCE OF ATTENTIVE LISTENING TO UNDERSTAND OTHERS' PERSPECTIVES.................83

        DEMONSTRATING RESPECT AND EMPATHY THROUGH VERBAL AND NON-VERBAL CUES.........87

        USING CLARIFYING QUESTIONS TO ENSURE A CLEAR UNDERSTANDING OF THE OTHER PERSON'S VIEWPOINT 91

    B.   BUILDING CREDIBILITY 95

        ESTABLISHING EXPERTISE THROUGH KNOWLEDGE AND EXPERIENCE 97

        HIGHLIGHTING SHARED VALUES OR COMMON GROUND 101

        PRESENTING ONESELF AS TRUSTWORTHY AND RELIABLE..105

    C.   EMOTIONAL APPEAL..109

        THE ROLE OF EMOTIONS IN DECISION-MAKING 113

        ELICITING EMOTIONS THROUGH STORYTELLING AND PERSONAL ANECDOTES.................117

        EMPATHY AND GENUINE CONCERN TO CREATE A MEANINGFUL CONNECTION 121

    D.   LOGICAL REASONING..125

STRUCTURING ARGUMENTS WITH CLEAR PREMISES AND CONCLUSIONS 129

PROVIDING EVIDENCE AND STATISTICS TO SUPPORT CLAIMS...133

ANTICIPATING COUNTERARGUMENTS AND ADDRESSING THEM EFFECTIVELY..........................137

E.   ETHICAL CONSIDERATIONS 141
HONESTY, TRANSPARENCY, AND INTEGRITY IN PERSUASIVE COMMUNICATION.....................145

RESPECTING THE AUTONOMY AND INDIVIDUAL RIGHTS OF OTHERS 147

RECOGNIZING AND AVOIDING MANIPULATION OR COERCION 151

III.   APPLICATION OF PERSUASION AND EFFECTIVE COMMUNICATION 157

A.   PERSUASION IN MARKETING AND ADVERTISING 161
UTILIZING PERSUASIVE TECHNIQUES TO INFLUENCE CONSUMER BEHAVIOR..........................165

MANIPULATION AND ETHICS IN MARKETING STRATEGIES...169

CREATING ETHICAL ADVERTISING THAT RESPECTS CONSUMER AUTONOMY 173

B.   PERSUASION IN POLITICAL COMMUNICATION 177
POLITICAL CAMPAIGNS AND THE ART OF PERSUASIVE MESSAGING 181

ETHICAL CONSIDERATIONS IN POLITICAL PERSUASION: TRUTHFULNESS AND FAIRNESS 185

ENSURING INFORMED DECISION-MAKING THROUGH UNBIASED DISSEMINATION OF
INFORMATION 189

C.   PERSUASION IN INTERPERSONAL RELATIONSHIPS...193
BUILDING SUCCESSFUL RELATIONSHIPS THROUGH EFFECTIVE COMMUNICATION 197

EMPATHY, ACTIVE LISTENING, AND COMPROMISE IN INTERPERSONAL PERSUASION.............201

THE IMPORTANCE OF ETHICAL PERSUASION IN FOSTERING TRUST AND MUTUAL RESPECT ..205

IV.   CONCLUSION 211

THE ART OF PERSUASION, PSYCHOLOGY BEHIND IT, AND EFFECTIVE COMMUNICATION
TECHNIQUES 213
ETHICAL CONSIDERATIONS IN PERSUASION ACROSS VARIOUS CONTEXTS 217

BIBLIOGRAPHY 223

INTRODUCTION

Effective persuasion and communication are essential skills in many aspects of life, ranging from personal relationships to professional success. Understanding the psychology behind persuasion and employing ethical techniques can greatly enhance one's ability to influence others. Whether it is in sales, politics, or everyday conversations, the art of persuasion plays a significant role in achieving desired outcomes. This essay will explore the various psychological principles that underlie persuasion and effective communication, with a focus on ethical approaches in different contexts. By delving into the intricacies of human behavior and the techniques employed to shape opinions, we can develop a comprehensive understanding of how to ethically persuade others while maintaining authenticity and respecting their autonomy. Persuasion, at its core, involves convincing others to adopt a particular idea, attitude, or behavior. The mere act of presenting an argument or making a request is insufficient to achieve persuasive success. Understanding the psychology of persuasion can illuminate the underlying mechanisms that drive human decision-making and enable individuals to communicate their message effectively. Numerous psychological theories, such as social influence, cognitive dissonance, and the elaboration likelihood model, provide valuable insights into the complexities of human receptivity to persuasive messages.

One influential theory in the field of persuasion is the concept of social influence. Social influence refers to the process through which people's thoughts, feelings, and behaviors are shaped by others in their social environment. This theory highlights the power of conformity and the desire to be accepted by others, emphasizing the importance of group norms and social expectations in the persuasion process. By understanding the principles of social influence, persuaders can tailor their message to align with the values and beliefs of their target audience, increasing the likelihood of acceptance and compliance.

Cognitive dissonance is another psychological principle that plays a significant role in persuasion. Cognitive dissonance occurs when individuals experience discomfort or tension due to holding conflicting beliefs or attitudes. This discomfort motivates individuals to reduce the dissonance by either changing their beliefs or justifying their current attitudes. Persuaders can leverage cognitive dissonance by presenting information that challenges the audience's existing beliefs, creating a sense of discrepancy. By highlighting the inconsistencies in their current attitudes, persuaders can motivate individuals to reconsider their position and ultimately align with the presented message.

The elaboration likelihood model (ELM) provides a framework for understanding how individuals process and evaluate persuasive messages based on their level of motivation and cognitive elaboration. According to the ELM, there are two routes to persuasion: the central route and the peripheral route. The central route involves a detailed analysis of the message arguments, with a focus on the logic and evidence presented. On the other hand, the peripheral route relies on heuristics, such as source attractiveness or the use of emotional appeals, to assess the message's credibility. By understanding the diverse ways in which individuals engage with persuasive messages, persuaders can tailor their approach to match the audience's level of motivation and cognitive elaboration, thereby increasing the likelihood of successful persuasion. While understanding the psychology behind persuasion is essential, it is equally important to approach persuasion ethically and responsibly. Ethics form the ethical boundaries that govern persuasive practices, ensuring that individuals are not manipulated or coerced into making decisions against their will. Ethical persuasion requires respecting the autonomy and individuality of others, promoting transparency, and avoiding deceptive or manipulative tactics. By adhering to ethical guidelines, persuaders can establish trust and credibility, fostering long-term relationships and positive outcomes.

Effective communication requires more than just understanding psychological principles and employing ethical techniques. It also necessitates the consideration of context. Different contexts, such as professional settings, interpersonal relationships, and political discourse, require distinct approaches to persuasion. Tailoring the message to suit the context can make it salient and relatable to the audience, increasing the likelihood of successful persuasion. For instance, in a professional setting, emphasizing the practical benefits and tangible outcomes of a proposal may carry more weight, whereas, in interpersonal relationships, appealing to emotions and personal values might be more effective. The art of persuasion involves understanding the psychology underlying human decision-making, employing ethical techniques, and tailoring the message to suit the context. By combining these elements, persuaders can enhance their ability to influence others ethically. Theories such as social influence, cognitive dissonance, and the elaboration likelihood model provide valuable insights into the mechanisms underlying persuasion. Ethical considerations must underpin all persuasive efforts to maintain authenticity, respect autonomy, and enable informed decision-making.

Becoming an effective persuader requires a comprehensive understanding of human behavior and communication, allowing individuals to navigate different contexts successfully and achieve desired outcomes.

THE ART OF PERSUASION: HOW TO INFLUENCE OTHERS ETHICALLY

The art of persuasion is a powerful tool that can be used to influence others ethically. It requires an understanding of the psychology of persuasion and the ability to communicate effectively in different contexts. Persuasion is the act of convincing someone to adopt a particular belief or take a specific action. It is a skill that is often utilized in various social, professional, and political settings. It is important to approach persuasion ethically, ensuring that the process respects the autonomy and well-being of the individuals involved. To be successful in persuasion, one must understand the psychological factors that influence human behavior and utilize effective communication techniques accordingly.

Understanding the psychology of persuasion is crucial in order to effectively influence others in an ethical manner. Persuasion is deeply rooted in human psychology, as it taps into the cognitive processes and biases that shape our decision-making. One important psychological principle is that of social proof, which suggests that individuals are more likely to adopt a certain belief or behavior if they see others doing the same. This can be observed in numerous social settings, such as the influence of peer pressure on adolescent behavior. By presenting examples or testimonials from individuals who have already adopted the desired belief or behavior, persuaders can leverage the power of social proof to increase the likelihood of persuasion.

Another influential psychological factor is that of reciprocity. Humans have a natural tendency to reciprocate favors or gestures, even in the absence of a pre-existing relationship. This principle can be utilized in persuasion by offering something of value to the target individual before making a request. By creating a sense of indebtedness, the persuader increases the likelihood that the individual will comply with their request. It is important to employ this technique ethically, ensuring that the favor or gesture offered is genuine and not manipulative.

Effective communication is also crucial in the art of persuasion. It involves conveying ideas and information in a clear and compelling manner that resonates with the target audience. One key aspect of effective communication is the ability to empathize with the concerns and perspectives of the individuals being persuaded. By understanding their values, beliefs, and motivations, persuaders can tailor their message to better resonate with the target audience. This requires active listening and the ability to adapt one's communication style to different contexts.

The use of logical arguments and evidence can greatly enhance persuasion. Humans are rational beings who are more likely to be persuaded by logical reasoning and evidence-based claims. Persuaders can strengthen their arguments by using facts, statistics, and expert opinions to support their claims.

It is important to present this information in a manner that is easily understandable and relatable to the target audience. Complex information should be broken down into simpler terms and presented in a compelling narrative that resonates with the emotions of the individuals being persuaded.

Context plays a major role in effective persuasion. Different contexts require different approaches to communication and persuasion. For instance, persuading someone in a formal professional setting requires a more formal and structured approach, whereas persuading someone in an informal social setting may require a more casual and conversational style. Similarly, persuading individuals from different cultural backgrounds or age groups may require a nuanced understanding of their specific values and communication preferences. Adapting one's persuasion techniques to different contexts is essential to ensure the message is received and understood by the target audience.

The art of persuasion involves understanding the psychology of persuasion and employing effective communication techniques in various contexts. Persuasion requires an ethical approach that prioritizes the autonomy and well-being of the individuals being influenced. By understanding the psychological factors that influence human behavior and leveraging effective communication techniques, persuaders can increase their chances of success. It is important to note that persuasion should always be used ethically and responsibly, with respect for the autonomy and well-being of those being persuaded. In order to understand the art of persuasion and its ethical implications, it is crucial to delve into the psychology of persuasion and the role of effective communication in different contexts. Persuasion is an integral part of human interaction, as it allows individuals to express their opinions, influence others, and initiate action. When employed unethically or manipulatively, persuasion can become a tool of deceit, exploitation, and harm. Understanding the psychological mechanisms underlying persuasion and tailoring communication techniques to promote ethical outcomes is vital for effective and responsible persuasion. One of the most influential theories on persuasion is the elaboration likelihood model (ELM), developed by Petty and Cacioppo (1986). According to this model, individuals engage in two cognitive processes when encountering persuasive messages: central route processing and peripheral route processing. Central route processing involves deep cognitive elaboration, where individuals carefully analyze the content, quality, and argumentative strength of the message. This type of processing is more likely to lead to enduring attitude change and behavioral effects. In contrast, peripheral route processing relies on heuristics and superficial cues, such as the credibility of the source or the attractiveness of the communicator. This type of processing is more susceptible to fleeting changes in attitudes and behavior. Understanding the ELM is crucial for crafting persuasive messages that are ethical and effective. When individuals engage in central route processing, it is essential to provide strong and credible arguments, present information in a clear and logical manner, and anticipate possible counterarguments. This approach aims to facilitate critical thinking and rational evaluation of the message, enhancing the likelihood of genuine attitude change. On the other hand, when peripheral route processing dominates, persuasive messages should focus on peripheral cues such as source attractiveness or likability. It is essential to ensure that these peripheral cues are relevant to the message and do not manipulate the audience's emotions or cognitive biases. By tailoring persuasive messages according to the ELM, one can ethically influence others while respecting their autonomy and rational decision-making processes. Effective communication is another crucial aspect of ethical persuasion. Communication is a complex process that involves encoding information, transmitting it via a channel, and decoding it by the intended audience. To maximize the effectiveness of persuasive communication, it is essential to consider various factors, such as the clarity of the message, the medium of communication, and the characteristics of the audience. Clarity is vital to ensure that the intended message is accurately transmitted and understood by the audience. Ambiguity or vagueness can lead to misinterpretation or confusion, undermining the effectiveness of persuasion. The medium of communication also significantly impacts persuasive outcomes. In today's digital age, various mediums, such as social media, websites, or email, provide platforms for persuasive communication. Each medium has its unique characteristics and limitations that influence how messages are received and interpreted. For example, social media platforms may reduce the complexity of messages and require concise, attention-grabbing content to capture the audience's fleeting attention. On the other hand, long-form articles or academic papers may provide more in-depth and detailed information, appealing to audiences who engage in central route processing. By identifying the appropriate medium and tailoring the message accordingly, persuasive communication can be made more effective and ethical. Understanding the characteristics and needs of the audience is paramount in ethical persuasion. Different individuals possess different beliefs, attitudes, and values that shape their responses to persuasive messages. Employing a one-size-fits-all approach is not effective or ethical. Instead, employing empathetic listening, observing nonverbal cues, and conducting audience analysis can provide insights into the specific needs, motivations, and biases of the target audience. By tailoring the persuasive message to resonate with the audience's values and addressing their concerns, ethical persuasion becomes more persuasive and respectful. The art of persuasion requires a comprehensive understanding of the psychology behind it and the role of effective communication in different contexts. The elaboration likelihood model elucidates the two cognitive processes individuals engage in when encountering persuasive messages, central route processing and peripheral route processing. Tailoring persuasive messages according to these processes ensures ethical and effective persuasion. Effective communication is crucial in encoding and decoding persuasive messages. Clarity, appropriate medium selection, and understanding the audience's characteristics and needs enhance the efficacy and ethics of persuasion. By utilizing these insights, individuals can ethically influence others and foster positive attitudes and behaviors, without resorting to manipulation or deceit.

DEFINITION OF PERSUASION, ITS IMPORTANCE, AND ITS ETHICAL IMPLICATIONS

In addition to understanding the psychological mechanisms behind persuasion, it is crucial to recognize its ethical implications. Persuasion can be a powerful tool that allows individuals or organizations to influence others' attitudes, beliefs, and behaviors. This influence comes with a responsibility to ensure that it is conducted ethically, without manipulation or coercion, in order to maintain trust and uphold moral standards. Ethical persuasion involves respecting the autonomy and free choice of others, providing accurate and reliable information, and considering the potential consequences of the persuasive message.

One of the main ethical considerations in persuasion is the respect for autonomy. Each individual should have the freedom to make their own choices and decide what is best for themselves. Ethical persuasion respects this autonomy by providing individuals with sufficient information and allowing them to make informed decisions. It does not rely on manipulative tactics or appeals to emotions to force individuals into believing a certain viewpoint or acting in a particular way. Instead, it focuses on presenting persuasive arguments that are based on logical reasoning and appeals to rationality. By respecting autonomy, ethical persuasion recognizes and values the individual's right to make their own choices and fosters a sense of empowerment rather than coercion. Another crucial aspect of ethical persuasion is the importance of providing accurate and reliable information. Persuasive messages should be founded on truthful and relevant facts, as well as valid and trustworthy sources. Misleading or false information can not only lead to negative consequences for the recipients but also undermine the integrity of the persuader. For instance, when a politician uses deceptive tactics to persuade voters, it not only manipulates the democratic process but also erodes the public's trust in the political system. In contrast, ethical persuasion prioritizes accuracy and honesty, recognizing that truthful information is essential for individuals to make informed decisions. By prioritizing truthfulness, ethical persuasion ensures that the process is transparent and builds trust between the persuader and the audience. Considering the potential consequences of persuasive messages is another vital ethical consideration. Persuasion can have both positive and negative effects, depending on how it is implemented. Ethical persuasion takes into account the potential harm or benefits that may arise from the persuasive message. It assesses the impact on individuals or groups and strives to minimize any potential harm while maximizing the potential benefits. Ethical persuasion is mindful of the long-term effects of the persuasive message and aims to promote well-being and social progress. For instance, when pharmaceutical companies engage in persuasive advertising, it is essential for them to consider the potential side effects of their drugs and ensure that the benefits outweigh the risks. By reflecting on the consequences, ethical persuasion ensures that the persuasive message aligns with the greater good and societal well-being.

It is also important to note that the context in which persuasion occurs plays a significant role in determining its ethical implications. Persuasion in a business context, for example, may involve convincing potential customers to purchase a product or service. Ethical persuasion in this setting entails providing accurate information about the product's features, benefits, and potential limitations. It also involves respecting the customer's autonomy by not pressuring or manipulating them into making a purchase against their will. In contrast, persuasion in a political context aims to influence public opinion and decision-making processes. Ethical persuasion in politics demands honest communication, providing well-founded arguments and engaging in respectful debate rather than resorting to deception or personal attacks. By recognizing the context in which persuasion occurs, ethical standards are tailored to specific situations, ensuring that the persuasive process adheres to moral principles and societal norms. Persuasion is a powerful tool that can shape attitudes, beliefs, and behaviors of individuals. It is essential to understand the psychological mechanisms behind persuasion, but equally important is the recognition of its ethical implications. Ethical persuasion involves respecting autonomy, providing accurate and reliable information, and considering the potential consequences of persuasive messages. By upholding these ethical principles, persuasion can be conducted in an ethical manner, building trust, and fostering empowerment. Ethical persuasion acknowledges the importance of context in determining its ethical implications, ensuring that the persuasive process adheres to moral principles and societal norms. Awareness of the ethical considerations of persuasion enables individuals and organizations to influence others effectively while maintaining integrity and promoting social progress. Thesis statement: The art of persuasion requires understanding the psychology behind it and employing effective communication techniques in different contexts.

In addition to understanding the psychology behind persuasion, another critical component is the utilization of effective communication techniques in various contexts. The art of persuasion is not a one-size-fits-all approach, as different situations call for different techniques. One such technique is the use of storytelling. Stories have been a fundamental part of human culture for centuries, and their power to captivate and influence an audience is unrivaled. By incorporating relevant and relatable stories into a persuasive message, one can evoke emotions and engage the audience on a deeper level. The use of visuals can greatly enhance the persuasiveness of a message. Visuals, such as graphs, charts, and images, have the ability to simplify complex information and make it more accessible to the audience. Visual aids not only make the message more memorable, but they also facilitate the audience's understanding, making them more likely to be persuaded. Another technique that can be employed in persuasive communication is the use of social proof. People tend to be influenced by the actions of others, especially those they perceive as similar to themselves. By providing evidence of others who have already adopted the desired behavior or belief, one can tap into the principle of social proof and increase the likelihood that the audience will follow suit. It is worth noting that the use of social proof should be done ethically and responsibly, as misusing it can lead to manipulation and exploitation. The context in which persuasion takes place plays a crucial role in the success of the persuasive message. Different contexts have different dynamics and require different strategies. For instance, persuading in a formal business setting may require a more logical and evidence-based approach, whereas persuading in a social setting may call for a more emotional and personal appeal. Understanding the cultural nuances and norms of a particular context is vital to effective persuasion. Different cultures have different values, beliefs, and communication styles, and tailoring the persuasive message to align with these cultural factors can significantly enhance its persuasiveness. The art of persuasion requires not only an understanding of the psychology behind it but also the skillful application of effective communication techniques in different contexts. Incorporating storytelling, utilizing visuals, leveraging social proof, and adapting to the specific context are all key elements in successfully persuading an audience. Persuasion is a powerful tool, and when used with ethical intent, it can create positive change and influence others in meaningful ways. By continually refining and honing our persuasive abilities, we can become not only more effective communicators but also more responsible and ethical influencers. In the modern world, where information is readily available and individuals are constantly bombarded with messages from various sources, the ability to persuade and influence others has become a vital skill. The art of persuasion, when employed ethically, can be a powerful tool for creating positive change and building harmonious relationships. To effectively persuade others, it is crucial to have a deep understanding of the psychology of persuasion and to employ effective communication strategies tailored to different contexts.

One key principle in the psychology of persuasion is social proof. According to Robert Cialdini, a renowned social psychologist, individuals are more likely to be influenced by the actions and behaviors of others. This theory stems from the innate human need for social validation and the tendency to conform to social norms. By leveraging the power of social proof, persuaders can effectively influence others to align their behavior or beliefs with a desired outcome. For example, marketing campaigns often utilize testimonials or endorsements from satisfied customers to create a sense of social proof and influence potential buyers.

Another important principle of persuasion is reciprocity. Humans have an innate tendency to reciprocate when they receive something beneficial. This principle can be harnessed in persuasive situations by providing individuals with a small favor or gift before making a request. This act of reciprocity creates a feeling of indebtedness, increasing the likelihood of compliance with subsequent requests. It is crucial that the gift or favor is genuine and not perceived as manipulative. In order to be ethical persuaders, it is essential to have the best interests of others at heart and not exploit their vulnerability. Understanding the concept of authority is crucial when aiming to persuade others. People are more likely to comply with requests that come from individuals perceived as authoritative figures. This perception is often influenced by factors such as titles, position in a hierarchy, or expertise in a specific field. To ethically employ the principle of authority, persuaders must establish their credibility and competence in the relevant domain before attempting to influence others. By utilizing their knowledge and expertise, persuaders can effectively convince others of the validity and importance of their proposals.

In addition to the psychological principles of persuasion, effective communication strategies play a crucial role in influencing others. One widely acknowledged method is the use of storytelling. Stories have a profound impact on individuals as they engage emotions, capture attention, and make information more memorable. When aiming to persuade, incorporating compelling narratives that resonate with the audience's experiences and values can significantly enhance the effectiveness of the message. By creating an emotional connection through storytelling, persuaders are more likely to engage the audience and elicit the desired response. Tailoring the communication style to different contexts is essential for successful persuasion. Persuasive messages that may be effective in one setting may not necessarily work in another. For instance, a direct and assertive approach may be effective when trying to influence a group of confident and ambitious individuals, while a more collaborative and empathetic approach may be required when persuading a team working on a collective project. Skilled persuaders have the ability to adapt their communication style to the specific needs and preferences of their audience, increasing their chances of success.

Ethical persuasion should prioritize long-term benefits over short-term gains. An effective persuader understands the importance of building trust and maintaining positive relationships. When employing persuasive strategies, it is crucial to avoid manipulation or deception that may result in short-lived compliance but damage relationships in the long run. By fostering genuine empathy and understanding, persuaders can create a foundation built on mutual respect and trust, laying the groundwork for ethical influence and long-term cooperation.

The art of persuasion relies on a deep understanding of the psychology of persuasion and effective communication strategies. By leveraging principles such as social proof, reciprocity, and authority, persuaders can ethically influence others and create positive change. Employing storytelling and tailoring communication styles to different contexts enhances the effectiveness of persuasive messages. It is of utmost importance to prioritize long-term benefits and maintain ethical standards when seeking to persuade others. With the proper knowledge and ethical approach,

the art of persuasion becomes a valuable tool for fostering har-
mony and creating meaningful connections in various spheres of
life.

I. THE PSYCHOLOGY OF PERSUASION

In addition to understanding the various techniques and principles of persuasion, it is important to delve into the psychology behind it. Persuasion is not just about presenting arguments in a convincing manner; it also involves understanding the cognitive and emotional processes that influence decision-making.

One key element of persuasion is cognitive dissonance, which refers to the discomfort people feel when they hold inconsistent beliefs or attitudes. According to Leon Festinger's theory, people are motivated to reduce this dissonance by either changing their beliefs or justifying their actions. This knowledge can be effectively applied in persuasive communication by helping individuals recognize any inconsistencies between their current beliefs and the desired action. By subtly highlighting such discrepancies, persuaders can motivate individuals to think critically and potentially change their attitudes or behavior. Another psychological factor that plays a significant role in persuasion is the principle of social proof. People tend to rely on information or cues from others when making decisions, especially in ambiguous situations. Robert Cialdini's research has shown that individuals are more likely to comply with a request if they believe others have also done so. This concept can be exploited in persuasive communication by highlighting the social popularity or credibility of a particular product, idea, or behavior. By showcasing testimonials, endorsements, or statistics about how many people have already adopted the desired action, persuaders can enhance the perceived validity and desirability of their message. Gaining a deep understanding of the target audience's emotions is crucial for effective persuasion. Emotionally charged messages are more likely to grab attention and evoke strong responses. It is important to note that deeper emotional engagement does not necessarily lead to persuasion. Instead, the emotions must be strategically harnessed to align with the persuasive message. For instance, positive emotions such as joy or excitement can be harnessed to associate positive feelings with the desired action or behavior. On the other hand, negative emotions such as fear or guilt can also be used to highlight potential negative consequences of not adhering to the persuasive message. The key is to strike the right balance between emotional impact and rational reasoning. Understanding the role of credibility and trust is essential in persuasive communication. People are more likely to be persuaded by individuals or sources they perceive as credible and trustworthy. Cialdini's expertise principle suggests that individuals are more willing to comply with requests from authorities or experts in a particular field. This principle can be leveraged by ensuring that the persuader is seen as knowledgeable, experienced, and trustworthy. Building trust through open and honest communication, providing evidence and logical reasoning, and demonstrating empathy towards the audience's concerns and perspectives can increase the credibility of the persuasive message. Finally, effective persuasion also requires effective communication skills. Persuasive messages should be clear, concise, and compelling. The use of rhetorical devices, such as storytelling, metaphors, or vivid imagery, can engage the audience and make the message more memorable. Active listening skills and the ability to adapt the message to the specific needs and concerns of the audience can enhance persuasiveness. Understanding the psychology behind persuasion is crucial for ethical influence. By aligning with the cognitive and emotional processes that shape decision-making, persuaders can create messages that resonate with their target audience. They can leverage cognitive dissonance to promote critical thinking and attitude change, utilize social proof to harness the power of social influence, tap into emotions to engage and motivate, and build credibility and trust through effective communication. The art of persuasion lies in the ability to ethically and skillfully sway others towards a desired outcome, while respecting their autonomy and empowering them to make informed decisions.

A. PRINCIPLES OF PERSUASION

In order to effectively influence others, it is important to understand the principles of persuasion. These principles, as outlined by Robert Cialdini in his book "Influence: The Psychology of Persuasion," provide valuable insights into the psychology behind why people say yes to certain requests or ideas. The first principle is reciprocity, which suggests that individuals feel obligated to give back to others who have given to them. By providing value or favors to others, one can create a sense of indebtedness and increase the likelihood of them complying with future requests. This principle can be seen in action when a salesperson offers a free sample or a small gift to a potential customer, making them feel obliged to reciprocate by purchasing the product. The second principle is scarcity, which states that people tend to place higher value on things that are rare or limited in availability. By highlighting the uniqueness or exclusivity of a product or idea, one can create a sense of urgency and heightened desire. This principle can be seen in action during limited-time promotions or when a product is marketed as being in short supply. The third principle is authority, which emphasizes that individuals are more likely to follow the advice or recommendations of knowledgeable or credible figures. By leveraging authority figures or experts in a particular field, one can enhance their own credibility and persuade others to adopt their viewpoint. This principle can be seen in action when doctors endorse certain medications or when celebrities promote a particular brand. The fourth principle is consistency, which suggests that people have a strong desire to be consistent with their past behaviors, beliefs, or commitments. By gaining initial agreement or commitment from others, one can increase the likelihood of them sticking to their original decision and complying with subsequent requests. This principle can be seen in action when someone signs a petition or makes a small donation to a cause, making them more likely to support larger initiatives in the future. The fifth principle is liking, which involves building rapport and establishing a positive connection with others. People are generally more willing to comply with requests from individuals they know, like, and trust. By finding commonalities and similarities with others, one can create a likeability factor that increases the chances of persuasion. This principle can be seen in action when salespeople engage in small talk or establish personal connections with potential customers. The final principle is consensus, which suggests that people tend to look to others for guidance when making decisions, especially in ambiguous or uncertain situations. By highlighting the popularity or widespread acceptance of a particular product or idea, one can create a sense of social proof and increase the likelihood of compliance. This principle can be seen in action when testimonials or customer reviews are used to promote a product or when companies advertise themselves as being the number one choice of customers. These principles of persuasion provide a framework for understanding how to ethically influence others and can be applied across a wide range of contexts, from sales and marketing to politics and negotiations. By incorporating these principles into our persuasive communication, we can enhance our effectiveness and achieve desired outcomes while maintaining ethical standards and respect for others.

RECIPROCITY: THE POWER OF GIVING AND RECEIVING

One key principle of persuasion is reciprocity, the power of giving and receiving. Reciprocity is a fundamental aspect of human social interaction that plays a crucial role in influencing others ethically. When someone does a favor or provides some kind of assistance, individuals often feel obligated to reciprocate. This social norm is deeply ingrained in our society and can be traced back to our evolutionary history. We are hardwired to feel a sense of indebtedness when someone is kind or helpful to us, as reciprocating such acts increases our chances of survival and social acceptance. Reciprocity serves as a powerful tool in the art of persuasion. By giving something of value to others, such as information, resources, or acts of kindness, individuals are more likely to gain compliance and influence. This principle is based on the persuasive technique known as the "door-in-the-face" strategy. According to this technique, when a large and unreasonable request is made initially, individuals are more likely to comply with a subsequent, smaller request. This approach leverages the power of reciprocity as the individual feels obligated to meet the smaller request to repay the perceived generosity of the requester. By skillfully manipulating the reciprocity norm, persuaders can influence others to meet their desired objectives.

Reciprocity has been studied extensively in both laboratory and real-world settings. Research has consistently demonstrated the persuasive effects of reciprocity. In one classic study conducted by Dennis Regan, participants engaged in a seemingly unrelated task with a confederate. During the task, the confederate would leave the room and return with two bottles of soda—one for the participant and one for themselves. In the experimental condition, the confederate would leave the room a second time, only to return empty-handed, claiming they had run out of soda for the participant. In the control condition, the confederate did not bring any soda in the first place. The results showed that participants who had received a soda from the confederate were significantly more likely to comply with a subsequent request—from buying raffle tickets to completing a survey—compared to those who did not receive a soda. This study highlights the power of reciprocity in influencing subsequent behavior.

It is essential to consider the ethics of utilizing reciprocity to persuade others. While reciprocity can be an effective tool, it should be used ethically and responsibly. Exploiting the reciprocity norm purely for personal gain or manipulating others into compliance undermines the ethical principles of persuasion. Persuasive communication should be rooted in transparency, honesty, and respect for others' autonomy. When employing reciprocity, persuaders should genuinely have the best interests of others in mind, and their requests should be reasonable and fair. If reciprocity is used manipulatively or unethically, the effects can undermine trust and damage relationships.

Reciprocity is a universal principle that transcends cultural boundaries. The manifestation of reciprocity norms may differ across cultures. In some cultures, reciprocity may be expressed through the exchange of gifts, while in others, it may involve acts of service or even indirect reciprocity, where the favor is returned to someone other than the initial benefactor. Cultural understanding is crucial when applying reciprocity to persuasion strategies. What may be perceived as a persuasive act in one culture could be seen as a bribe or manipulation in another. Effective communicators must adapt their approach accordingly and respect cultural nuances. Reciprocity is a powerful principle in the art of persuasion. By giving something of value, individuals can leverage the sense of indebtedness in others and influence their behavior. It is essential to approach reciprocity ethically and responsibly, ensuring that requests are fair and align with principles of transparency and respect. Reciprocity is a universal norm, but its expression may vary across cultures, necessitating a culturally sensitive approach. The art of persuasion with reciprocity lies in understanding the psychology behind it and using it to foster positive relationships and achieve mutual benefits.

SOCIAL PROOF: THE INFLUENCE OF OTHERS' ACTIONS ON OUR DECISION-MAKING

Social proof is a powerful tool that can greatly impact our decision-making. It is the concept that suggests people will conform to the actions of others under the assumption that those actions are reflective of the correct behavior in a given situation. This phenomenon is deeply rooted in our human nature, as we are inherently social beings who seek acceptance and validation from our peers. When we see others engaging in a particular behavior, we are more likely to follow suit, as it provides us with a sense of belonging and conformity within our social groups. The influence of social proof extends beyond simply wanting to fit in; it also stems from the belief that the actions of others provide us with valuable information in uncertain or ambiguous situations. We often look to others to guide our actions, as we instinctively assume that if numerous people are engaging in a behavior, it must be the correct course of action. This is particularly evident in situations where we lack personal knowledge or experience, causing us to rely on the experiences and judgments of others. This reliance on social proof can be seen in numerous aspects of our daily lives, including product choices, voting decisions, and even emergency situations. For example, when deciding on which product to purchase, we often look to customer reviews or seek recommendations from friends and family. The positive experiences and opinions of others can serve as a form of social proof, providing us with the reassurance and confidence to make a particular choice. Similarly, in the realm of politics, the opinions of our peers can significantly influence our voting decisions. We may be inclined to support a particular candidate if we see that they have a strong backing from others, as it reinforces the notion that this candidate is the popular and favorable choice. Social proof can play a crucial role in emergency situations. When faced with a crisis, we look to the reactions and actions of those around us for guidance on how to respond. This can be seen in situations such as evacuations, where individuals are more likely to evacuate if they see others doing so. This reliance on social proof is often driven by the assumption that others possess greater knowledge or understanding of the situation, and that following their lead will lead to a better outcome. While social proof can be a powerful tool for persuasion and influence, it is important to recognize its potential pitfalls. The reliance on social proof can lead individuals to make decisions that do not align with their personal values or beliefs. This can result in a lack of critical thinking and a tendency to go along with the crowd, adopting behaviors or opinions simply because others are doing so. Social proof can be easily manipulated and exploited by those seeking to influence others for personal gain. For instance, marketers often employ tactics such as testimonials and celebrity endorsements to create the illusion of social proof and influence consumer behavior. This highlights the importance of being aware of the influence of social proof and exercising critical thinking when making decisions. Social proof serves as a powerful psychological force that can greatly impact our decision-making processes. It provides us with a sense of belonging and validation, while also offering guidance in uncertain or unfamiliar situations. It is crucial to approach social proof with caution and to engage in critical thinking to ensure that our decisions align with our personal values and beliefs. By understanding the influence of social proof and its potential pitfalls, we can navigate the art of persuasion and make decisions that are ethical and true to ourselves.

AUTHORITY: THE IMPACT OF PERCEIVED EXPERTISE OR AUTHORITY FIGURES

At its core, authority plays a significant role in persuasion and is often associated with expertise or credibility. When individuals perceive someone as an authority figure, they are more likely to be influenced by their words or actions. This impact of perceived authority can be seen in various contexts, such as the healthcare industry, education, and business. In the healthcare industry, for example, patients tend to listen to and adhere to the advice given by doctors or medical professionals due to their perceived expertise. This authority is built on a foundation of extensive knowledge and experience, and patients trust that these individuals have their best interests at heart. Similarly, in the realm of education, students are more likely to accept the guidance provided by their professors or teachers, viewing them as credible sources of information. In this context, the authority figure's qualifications, such as degrees or certifications, further enhance their perceived expertise. In the business world, authority figures such as CEOs or managers can use their position of power to influence the decisions and behaviors of their subordinates. Employees may feel compelled to comply with their superiors, believing that these individuals possess the necessary knowledge and experience to lead effectively. It is crucial to note that perceived authority can be misused and exploited for personal gain, which can lead to ethical concerns. Consequently, the impact of perceived expertise or authority figures in persuasion must be approached with caution and a strong emphasis on ethical behavior.

CONSISTENCY: THE DESIRE TO ALIGN WITH OUR PAST COMMITMENTS

Consistency is a powerful principle of persuasion that taps into our desire to align with our past commitments. As humans, we have a deep-rooted need for consistency, both in our thoughts and actions. This need stems from our desire to appear rational and stable individuals who possess integrity. When we commit to certain beliefs or behaviors, we are more likely to stick to them because inconsistency has negative connotations in society. People who are perceived as inconsistent are often seen as unreliable, lacking integrity, or even manipulative. Hence, consistency is not only a personal trait but a societal expectation.

In the realm of persuasion, harnessing the power of consistency allows individuals to influence others effectively. One way to leverage consistency is by using the foot-in-the-door technique, which begins with a small request or action that is designed to prime individuals for a larger commitment later on. This strategy operates on the premise that once an individual agrees to a small favor, they are more likely to comply with subsequent, more significant requests in order to maintain consistency.

For instance, many organizations use the foot-in-the-door technique to solicit donations. They may begin by requesting a small contribution, such as a few dollars, from potential donors. Once individuals agree to this initial request and make a donation, they are more likely to feel obligated to provide larger donations in the future. The logic behind this is that people want to maintain consistency in their actions. If they have already demonstrated a commitment to the cause, they are more likely to continue supporting it in order to align with their previous behavior.

Another strategy that capitalizes on consistency is the lowball technique. This technique involves presenting a tempting offer to individuals, which they readily accept. After they commit to the offer, additional costs or conditions are revealed. Despite the changes in the original offer, individuals are more likely to stick with their decision because they want to maintain consistency with their initial commitment. Car salespeople often use the lowball technique to persuade customers to make a purchase. They may initially offer an attractive price for a desired vehicle, only to later disclose additional costs for things like warranties or add-ons. By this point, individuals have already made the commitment to purchase the car and are more likely to accept the extra costs to maintain consistency with their initial decision. This approach exploits the psychological principle that people have a natural tendency to justify their commitments and avoid the discomfort associated with inconsistency.

Consistency also plays a crucial role in shaping our self-image and influencing our behavior. When we publicly commit to a belief or action, we are more likely to behave in ways that align with that commitment to maintain internal consistency. This phenomenon is known as the "commitment and consistency principle." For example, individuals who publicly proclaim their commitment to living a healthy lifestyle are more likely to engage in behaviors such as exercising regularly or eating nutritious foods. By openly declaring their dedication to health, individuals create a self-image that aligns with their commitment, and subsequently, feel compelled to act consistently with that image.

Consistency is not only a personal virtue but also a societal expectation. Consistency is highly valued in relationships, workplaces, and communities. People expect others to be consistent in their behaviors, actions, and words. Inconsistency is often perceived as a breach of trust and reliability. When someone behaves inconsistently, it raises doubts about their integrity and credibility. Conversely, consistent individuals are seen as dependable, trustworthy, and reliable. They are more likely to gain the respect and support of others, both personally and professionally. Consistency is a powerful principle of persuasion that taps into our desire to align with our past commitments. It is a psychological need that drives us to behave and think in a manner that is consistent with our previous actions. By leveraging consistency, individuals can ethically influence others, showcasing the foot-in-the-door technique and the lowball technique. Consistency also shapes our self-image and influences our behavior, as we strive to maintain internal consistency. Moreover, consistency is a societal expectation, with inconsistency often viewed as a breach of trust and reliability. Understanding and utilizing the principle of consistency can be a potent tool in effective communication and persuasion.

LIKING: THE INFLUENCE OF AFFECTION AND SIMILARITY ON PERSUASION

It is evident that liking plays a significant role in persuasion, as individuals are more likely to be persuaded by someone they like. Affection and similarity are two key factors that contribute to liking and ultimately impact the effectiveness of persuasion techniques. When an individual feels affection or a positive emotional connection towards a persuader, they are more inclined to be open-minded and receptive to their message. This emotional bond can be formed through various means, such as compliments, humor, or shared experiences. By establishing a positive rapport, the persuader can create a favorable attitude towards themselves, which in turn facilitates the acceptance of their persuasive message. Individuals are more likely to be persuaded by someone they perceive to be similar to themselves. When someone shares common interests, beliefs, or values, it creates a sense of familiarity and trust. This similarity increases the persuader's credibility and fosters a sense of identification with the audience. Consequently, individuals are more likely to internalize and act upon a persuasive message if they perceive the source as being similar to themselves. The influence of liking, through affection and similarity, highlights the importance of building positive relationships and finding common ground in the persuasion process.

SCARCITY: THE ALLURE OF LIMITED RESOURCES OR OPPORTUNITIES

Scarcity is a powerful persuasive technique that taps into people's innate fear of missing out. When something is in short supply or limited in availability, it automatically becomes more desirable. This principle of scarcity is deeply rooted in human psychology and can be seen in various contexts, from retail marketing to job interviews. Marketers often utilize scarcity by creating a sense of urgency and limited availability for their products. Limited-time offers, exclusive deals, and flash sales all play on the fear of missing out, prompting individuals to make impulsive purchases. Scarcity is also employed in the realm of job interviews. When a company presents a limited number of job openings, the competition among candidates intensifies, making each opportunity much more coveted. This scarcity principle creates a sense of urgency, motivating individuals to put in extra effort and stand out from the crowd. Scarcity can also be observed in social interactions, where individuals may perceive someone or something as more valuable if they believe it is scarce. For example, someone who is seen as "hard to get" might be more desirable than someone who is readily available. This concept is applicable in dating and relationship contexts, where individuals may be drawn to partners who are perceived as hard to attain due to their scarce availability or desirability. Scarcity is a powerful persuasive technique that taps into the innate fear of missing out and can be used effectively in various contexts to influence others ethically. The art of persuasion and effective communication relies on understanding the psychology behind why people act and make decisions. By incorporating these principles into our interactions, we can ethically influence others and create positive outcomes. Reciprocity allows individuals to feel a social obligation to return favors, while social proof leverages the power of conformity to influence behavior. Authority establishes credibility and trust, while consistency builds commitment and fosters a sense of identity. Liking creates rapport and makes individuals more open to persuasion, and scarcity taps into the innate fear of missing out to create desire. Understanding and applying these techniques in a responsible and ethical manner can enable individuals to navigate various contexts successfully and achieve desired results. Hence, mastering the art of persuasion is not just about gaining an upper hand over others, but rather, a tool for fostering meaningful connections, inspiring positive change, and influencing others in a way that respects their autonomy and values.

B. COGNITIVE BIASES

Cognitive biases, another crucial aspect of understanding persuasion and effective communication, refer to the systematic errors in thinking that individuals make when processing information. As humans, we possess limited cognitive resources and rely on efficient mental shortcuts or heuristics to navigate complex decision-making processes. These cognitive shortcuts can lead to biases that systematically distort our perceptions, judgments, and decision-making abilities. One prominent cognitive bias is the confirmation bias, which refers to our tendency to seek and interpret information in a way that confirms our pre-existing beliefs or hypotheses, while disregarding or discounting information that contradicts them. This bias not only affects how we perceive and understand the world, but also shapes our attitudes and influences the way we communicate with others. Another significant cognitive bias is the availability heuristic, where we tend to judge the likelihood of events based on how easily examples come to mind. For instance, if we can easily recall instances of car accidents, we are more likely to believe that car accidents are more common than they actually are. The availability heuristic can impact our perceptions of risk, as we may overestimate the probability of rare but highly publicized negative events, such as plane crashes or terrorist attacks. The anchoring bias is yet another cognitive bias that affects our decision-making processes. It occurs when individuals rely too heavily on the first piece of information they receive (the anchor) when making subsequent judgments or estimates. For example, if a car is originally listed for sale at a high price, subsequent negotiations may orbit around this initial figure, leading to a higher final selling price. This bias highlights the importance of setting appropriate anchors in persuasive communication, as they can significantly influence the outcome of negotiations or decisions.

The framing effect is a cognitive bias that demonstrates how the presentation or framing of information can affect our judgments and decision-making. People tend to be influenced by the way information is presented, even if the actual content is the same. For instance, individuals are more likely to choose a product if it is framed as "80% fat-free" rather than "contains 20% fat." This bias emphasizes the power of language and framing in influencing how individuals perceive and evaluate information. The overconfidence effect is a cognitive bias where individuals tend to have unwarranted confidence in their judgments and abilities, often overestimating their own knowledge, skills, or the accuracy of their predictions. This bias can impact the persuasiveness of an individual's communication, as overconfident speakers may come across as more competent and persuasive, even if their claims lack validity or evidence. Recognizing and understanding these cognitive biases is paramount in ethical persuasion and effective communication. By acknowledging these biases, individuals can be more mindful of their own thought processes and work towards making logical, well-reasoned decisions. Being aware of these biases allows individuals to critically evaluate the information they receive and determine whether it is reliable and accurate. For persuasive communicators, understanding cognitive biases can aid in crafting messages that are more persuasive by strategically appealing to individuals' cognitive shortcuts and biases. By leveraging the anchoring effect or framing information in a favorable manner, communicators can increase their chances of persuading their audience. It is essential to use these techniques ethically and responsibly, ensuring that the information presented is accurate and not deliberately manipulated to exploit individuals' cognitive biases. Recognizing and addressing cognitive biases can contribute to more effective communication by promoting open-mindedness, empathy, and the consideration of diverse perspectives. By actively challenging our own biases and seeking out alternative viewpoints, we can engage in meaningful conversations that foster mutual understanding and respect. Cognitive biases play a vital role in shaping our perceptions, judgments, and decision-making processes. As influential factors in persuasion and effective communication, they highlight the importance of understanding human psychology in various contexts. By acknowledging and addressing cognitive biases, individuals can enhance their own decision-making abilities, critically evaluate information, and engage in ethical persuasion. These biases underline the significance of responsible and mindful communication, emphasizing the need for communicators to respect their audience's rationality and avoid exploiting cognitive shortcuts for unethical purposes. Understanding cognitive biases not only aids individuals in navigating the complexities of persuasion, but also contributes to more effective and ethical communication practices.

CONFIRMATION BIAS

The tendency to interpret information in a way that confirms preexisting beliefs. Confirmation bias is a cognitive bias that refers to the tendency to interpret information in a way that confirms preexisting beliefs. It is a natural and unconscious process that affects individuals' decision-making and perception of reality. The human brain has a natural inclination to seek information that supports its existing beliefs and filters out contradictory evidence. This bias can be observed in various contexts, such as personal relationships, politics, and scientific research. In personal relationships, confirmation bias can lead individuals to selectively perceive and interpret information that confirms their beliefs about their partners. For example, someone who believes that their partner is untrustworthy may interpret innocent actions as evidence of betrayal, discounting any evidence to the contrary. Confirmation bias also plays a significant role in political discourse, where individuals tend to seek out and accept information that aligns with their political views while disregarding opposing perspectives. This bias can contribute to the creation of echo chambers, where people only engage with like-minded individuals and reinforce their preconceived notions. In the scientific domain, confirmation bias can hinder the pursuit of objective truth. Researchers who hold strong beliefs or vested interests in a particular outcome may unconsciously interpret and present data that confirms their hypothesis, while neglecting contradictory findings. This phenomenon is especially prevalent in controversial areas of research, where personal beliefs and funding sources may influence the interpretation of scientific data. Confirmation bias can have significant consequences on decision-making and the formation of beliefs. It can lead people to overlook alternative explanations or ignore valuable information that challenges their preexisting beliefs. This bias can perpetuate stereotypes, reinforce prejudices, and hinder open-mindedness. Confirmation bias may lead individuals to engage in motivated reasoning, where they actively seek out information that supports their beliefs and dismiss contradicting evidence. Over time, this can create a self-perpetuating cycle that prevents individuals from critically evaluating their beliefs and considering alternative perspectives. Recognizing and overcoming confirmation bias is crucial for effective communication and ethical persuasion. To mitigate the impact of confirmation bias, individuals should actively seek out diverse sources of information and expose themselves to alternative viewpoints. Engaging in respectful and open-minded discussions with people who hold different beliefs can expand one's perspective and challenge preexisting notions. Critical thinking skills, such as evaluating evidence and considering alternate explanations, can help individuals overcome confirmation bias and make more objective judgments. Promoting intellectual humility, the willingness to acknowledge and accept the fallibility of one's own beliefs, is also essential in combating confirmation bias. By recognizing that one's beliefs may be influenced by personal and cognitive biases, individuals can approach information with a more open and unbiased mindset. Confirmation bias is a natural tendency to interpret information in a way that confirms preexisting beliefs. It can affect decision-making processes, perceptions of reality, and the formation of beliefs. Confirmation bias is observed in various contexts, ranging from personal relationships to scientific research. It can lead to the creation of echo chambers, hinder the pursuit of truth, and perpetuate prejudices. Overcoming confirmation bias requires actively seeking out diverse perspectives, engaging in critical thinking, and promoting intellectual humility. Recognizing and addressing confirmation bias is crucial for effective communication and ethical persuasion.

ANCHORING BIAS: THE OVERRELIANCE ON INITIAL INFORMATION

Anchoring bias is a critical aspect of human psychology that greatly affects our decision-making processes. It refers to the tendency to rely too heavily on the initial information we receive when making judgments or decisions. This bias occurs when we anchor our thoughts and subsequent actions to the first piece of information presented to us, even if it may not be relevant or accurate. Anchoring bias has been extensively studied and has been found to have significant implications in various fields such as finance, marketing, and negotiation.

One example of anchoring bias can be observed in the context of pricing. Research has shown that consumers tend to rely heavily on the first price they encounter when making purchasing decisions. For instance, when presented with a high-priced luxury item, individuals may perceive the subsequent products as more reasonably priced, even if they are still expensive compared to alternatives. This anchoring effect can influence consumer behavior and lead to higher sales for businesses, as individuals may be willing to pay more than they initially intended due to the anchoring bias. Marketers often utilize this bias by displaying a higher-priced item before presenting the desired product, thus influencing consumers to perceive the latter as a better value for money. Anchoring bias also plays a significant role in negotiations. Studies have shown that the initial offer made in a negotiation can have a powerful anchoring effect on the final outcome. For example, if a seller starts with a high asking price, it can

anchor the buyer's perception of what is reasonable and acceptable. They may then find it challenging to counter with a significantly lower offer, even if it would be more appropriate given
market conditions. This anchoring bias can lead to suboptimal
agreements as individuals may be influenced by the initial anchor
rather than considering the actual value or fairness of the offer.
Negotiators who are aware of this bias can strategically use anchoring to their advantage by setting a higher anchor to secure a
more favorable position in the negotiation.

The anchoring bias also has implications in the financial realm.
Investors often anchor their valuation of stocks or other assets to
the initial price they paid. This anchoring effect can result in investors holding onto undervalued assets for an extended period,
expecting them to regain their initial value. This bias can lead to
poor investment decisions as individuals fail to update their valuation based on new information or market conditions. Academic
research has demonstrated that anchoring bias can influence an-
alysts' forecasts and market expectations, leading to price distortions and market inefficiencies.

Understanding anchoring bias is crucial to effective communication and persuasion. By recognizing the impact of the initial information presented, individuals can guard against being swayed
solely by this anchor and can make more rational judgments and
decisions. Being aware of anchoring biases can facilitate ethical
persuasion by avoiding manipulative techniques that exploit this
cognitive bias. There are several ways individuals can combat the
effects of anchoring bias. One approach is to consciously consider
alternative perspectives and information before accepting the initial anchor. By actively seeking out additional information, individuals can have a more well-rounded understanding of the

situation, reducing the influence of the initial anchor. Deliberating with others and engaging in discussions can help challenge and counterbalance the anchoring effect. By sharing different perspectives and challenging one another's assumptions, individuals can collectively make more informed decisions.

Self-awareness and critical thinking are key in overcoming anchoring bias. Individuals should reflect on their thinking processes and question whether they are unduly influenced by the initial anchor. By consciously monitoring their decision-making, individuals can become more aware of the biases that may be at play and take steps to counteract them. Developing the ability to adjust and update initial judgments based on new information is crucial to overcoming the anchoring bias.

Anchoring bias is a prevalent cognitive bias that affects our decision-making processes. It can result in overreliance on initial information, leading to suboptimal judgments and decisions. This bias is evident in various contexts, including pricing, negotiations, and financial decision-making. Being aware of anchoring bias and employing strategies to counteract its effects is essential for making rational decisions and engaging in ethical persuasion. By actively seeking additional information, deliberating with others, and being self-aware, individuals can mitigate the influence of anchoring bias and improve their decision-making abilities.

AVAILABILITY BIAS: THE TENDENCY TO RELY ON READILY AVAILABLE INFORMATION WHEN MAKING JUDGMENTS

Availability bias refers to the human tendency to rely on readily available information when making judgments. This bias can significantly impact decision-making processes, as people often overlook more accurate or relevant information that is not readily accessible. Individuals tend to recall information and experiences that are easily retrievable from their memory, often due to their vividness or frequency of exposure, leading to skewed judgments. For example, if a person has recently seen multiple news reports highlighting criminal activities in their neighborhood, they may overestimate the crime rate and feel unsafe, even if statistical data shows otherwise. Similarly, if a person has personally encountered a rare medical condition, they may assume it to be more prevalent than it actually is. Availability bias can occur due to various factors, including media influence, personal experiences, or even language usage. It is crucial to recognize and mitigate the effects of availability bias to make well-informed decisions. The impact of availability bias on decision-making extends beyond personal judgments and can have profound implications in various contexts. In advertising and marketing, companies leverage availability bias by repeatedly exposing consumers to their brand and messaging, making it more accessible in their memory. This accessibility can influence individuals' preferences and choices when faced with purchasing decisions. For instance, a consumer may gravitate towards a familiar brand due to the ease of recall and the perception that it is a more reliable option, even if there are better alternatives available. By understanding the psychology behind availability bias, advertisers can strategically design campaigns to increase brand recall and influence consumer behavior ethically. Availability bias can significantly affect policy-making and public opinion. Politicians and policymakers often exploit this bias by selectively highlighting vivid and emotionally charged examples to sway public opinion. Such examples create a sense of urgency and, by making them readily available in people's minds, influence their decision-making processes. For instance, in debates surrounding immigration policy, politicians may emphasize isolated incidents of criminal behavior committed by immigrants to evoke fear and justify stricter policies. By presenting these instances as representative of a larger group, availability bias can shape public perception and hinder an objective understanding of the issue. Recognizing the persuasive power of availability bias is crucial in evaluating policy proposals and fostering informed discussions. Availability bias can also impact interpersonal communication and relationships. In conversations and debates, individuals often rely on information that is easily accessible in their memory, leading to a narrow or incomplete perspective. This can result in misunderstandings and arguments rooted in incomplete or biased information. For example, if someone repeatedly hears negative opinions about a colleague, they may develop a biased perception of that individual, overlooking their positive qualities. Availability bias can hinder effective communication and collaboration as it limits the range of information considered, reinforcing pre-existing biases and preventing a more comprehensive understanding of others' perspectives. By consciously recognizing our tendency towards availability bias, we can strive to seek diverse and relevant information to foster healthy and open communication.

To mitigate the impact of availability bias, one should actively seek out diverse information and consider a broader range of perspectives. Critical thinking and analysis can help challenge readily available information and enable individuals to make more informed judgments. Engaging with different sources, assessing data and statistics, and questioning personal experiences can all contribute to a more balanced understanding of a situation. Slowing down the decision-making process can assist in overcoming availability bias. By taking the time to reflect and actively seek out alternative information, individuals can avoid falling into the trap of relying solely on readily available information.

Availability bias significantly influences decision-making processes by leading individuals to rely on readily available information. This bias can result in skewed judgments, overlooking relevant or more accurate data. Availability bias can be leveraged in advertising and marketing but also exploited in politics and policymaking to shape public opinion. In interpersonal communication, this bias may hinder understanding and lead to misunderstandings. Recognizing and actively mitigating availability bias is essential to ensure well-informed decision-making and foster effective communication and collaboration. By seeking diverse sources of information, engaging in critical thinking, and questioning personal experiences, individuals can overcome the limitations imposed by availability bias and approach decision-making with a more balanced perspective.

LOSS AVERSION: THE GREATER WEIGHT GIVEN TO POTENTIAL LOSSES OVER EQUIVALENT GAINS

Another important aspect of the psychology of persuasion is loss aversion, which refers to the tendency to place a greater weight on potential losses compared to equivalent gains. This phenomenon has significant implications for influencing others ethically. Research has shown that people are generally more motivated to avoid losses than to acquire equivalent gains. This can be attributed to the emotional impact of losses, which tend to elicit stronger negative emotions like fear and sadness. These negative emotions associated with potential losses heighten individuals' motivation to take action and prevent the loss from occurring. In contrast, the positive emotions associated with potential gains are typically less intense, leading to a lower motivation to act. Understanding this psychological bias is crucial for effectively persuading others, as it allows for the framing of messages that emphasize the potential losses that individuals may incur if they do not adopt a certain behavior or take a particular course of action. By highlighting the negative consequences of inaction, persuasive communicators can tap into individuals' loss aversion and increase the likelihood of their compliance. It is important to note that ethical persuasion requires a careful balance. While loss aversion can be a powerful tool, it should not be exploited to create undue fear or manipulate individuals into making decisions against their best interests. Instead, ethical communicators should present an accurate and balanced depiction of potential losses, while also offering viable solutions or alternatives to address these losses. A successful persuasive message is one that respects individuals' autonomy and provides them with the necessary information to make informed choices. Loss aversion can be leveraged to encourage positive behaviors and actions. By highlighting the potential gains that individuals stand to lose if they fail to adopt a desired behavior, communicators can effectively motivate them to take action. This strategy has been successfully employed in various domains, such as health promotion campaigns, where messages often emphasize the potential health risks individuals may face if they do not engage in healthy behaviors. For instance, anti-smoking campaigns often depict the detrimental effects of smoking, highlighting the potential loss of health and longevity that smokers may experience. By appealing to individuals' loss aversion, these campaigns aim to influence behavior change and encourage smokers to quit. Loss aversion plays a significant role in the psychology of persuasion and effective communication. By understanding and harnessing this bias, communicators can enhance their ability to influence others ethically. However, it is crucial to maintain ethical standards by avoiding manipulation and instead providing individuals with accurate information and viable alternatives. Ethical persuasion requires a genuine concern for individuals' autonomy and best interests, rather than solely focusing on achieving desired outcomes. By striking the right balance, communicators can leverage loss aversion to inspire positive action and facilitate behavior change, ultimately leading to more effective communication and better outcomes for all parties involved.

FRAMING EFFECT: THE INFLUENCE OF HOW INFORMATION IS PRESENTED OR FRAMED

The framing effect is a psychological phenomenon that highlights the profound influence of how information is presented or framed on individual decision-making processes. As human beings, we are constantly bombarded with information from various sources, and how this information is presented can greatly impact our perceptions and subsequent actions. The framing effect suggests that people tend to make different decisions based on the way information is framed, even if the content remains the same.

One classic example of the framing effect is the concept of gain versus loss framing. When information is presented in a gain frame, focusing on the positive aspects and potential benefits, individuals are more likely to take risks and make choices that maximize their gains. On the other hand, when information is presented in a loss frame, emphasizing the negative consequences and potential losses, people tend to be more risk-averse and opt for choices that minimize their losses. This can be seen in various contexts, such as marketing campaigns or political messaging, where framing the information in a positive or negative light can influence consumer behavior and public opinion.

Another form of framing effect is attribute framing, which focuses on presenting information in terms of different attributes or characteristics. When information is framed positively, highlighting the benefits and positive attributes of a particular option, people are more likely to be persuaded and make decisions based on those positive attributes. Conversely, when information is framed negatively, emphasizing the drawbacks and negative attributes, individuals may be more hesitant and reluctant to choose that option. Attribute framing can be seen in advertising, where products are often presented in a positive light, focusing on their desirable attributes to convince consumers to purchase them.

Framing effect can also be observed in the context of risk perception and communication. The way information about risks is framed can influence how individuals perceive and respond to those risks. For instance, research has shown that presenting information about the probability of an event occurring in terms of percentages can lead to different risk perceptions compared to presenting the same information in terms of frequencies. People tend to perceive risks as higher when information is presented using frequencies rather than probabilities.

The framing effect can also be observed in the context of health communication and decision-making. For example, research has shown that framing health messages in terms of gains or losses can significantly influence behavior change. Individuals may be more motivated to engage in healthy behaviors when the benefits of such behaviors are emphasized, whereas they may be more inclined to avoid unhealthy behaviors when the negative consequences are highlighted. This has implications for public health campaigns and interventions, as understanding how to effectively frame information can enhance the effectiveness of health communication and encourage positive behavior change.

It is important to acknowledge that while the framing effect can be a powerful tool for persuasion and communication, it also raises ethical concerns. The manipulation of information through framing techniques can potentially exploit individuals' cognitive biases and lead to decisions that are not in their best interest. It is crucial for communicators and persuaders to prioritize ethical practices and ensure that framing is used responsibly and transparently. The framing effect demonstrates how the presentation of information can significantly influence decision-making and behavior. Whether it is through gain versus loss framing, attribute framing, or risk framing, the way information is framed can shape our perceptions and responses. Understanding the psychology behind framing can help communicators, marketers, and policy-makers ethically influence others and effectively convey their messages. It is essential to recognize the ethical implications of framing and ensure that it is used in a responsible and transparent manner. As knowledge of the framing effect continues to evolve, further research and understanding will contribute to the development of more ethical and impactful persuasive strategies. The third principle of persuasion is social proof. People are more likely to be influenced by the actions of others, especially those they perceive to be similar to themselves. This is rooted in the human desire for conformity and a need for guidance in uncertain situations. When individuals are unsure of how to act or make decisions, they often look to others for social cues. This is evident in various aspects of our everyday lives, from the way we dress to the products we purchase. For example, when we see a celebrity endorsing a particular brand, we may be more inclined to believe that the product is of high quality and worth purchasing. Similarly, when we hear about a popular trend or see others engaging in a particular behavior, we are more likely to conform and adopt that behavior ourselves. This principle of influence is pervasive in marketing and advertising, where companies often use testimonials, endorsements, and celebrity spokespersons to show that others have had positive experiences with their products or services. By providing social proof, these companies are leveraging the power of influence and persuasion to sway consumers' decisions. Social proof can also be seen in the realm of social media, where individuals often look to the behavior and opinions of others before forming their own. The number of followers, likes, and comments that an individual receives on social media platforms can have a significant impact on their perceived credibility and influence. Social proof can extend beyond the digital world and into our personal lives. When we see our friends or family members engaging in certain activities or adopting certain beliefs, we are more likely to do the same. This is known as informational social influence, as we are using others' behavior as a source of information to guide our own decisions. It is important to note that social proof can be both positive and negative. While it can be a powerful tool for influencing others ethically, it can also be used to exploit vulnerabilities and manipulate people's behavior. For instance, in situations where individuals feel uncertain or unsure of themselves, they may be more susceptible to following the actions and opinions of others, even if they are not in their best interest. This highlights the importance of using social proof responsibly and ethically, ensuring that it is used to inform and empower rather than manipulate and deceive. The principle of social proof is a vital component of the art of persuasion. By leveraging the power of influence and conformity, individuals and organizations can effectively persuade and influence others' behavior. Understanding the psychology behind social proof can enhance our ability to communicate and resonate with others in different contexts, whether in marketing, advertising, or personal relationships. It is incumbent upon us to use social proof responsibly and ethically, ensuring that it benefits the well-being and autonomy of those we seek to influence. By harnessing the psychology of persuasion and effective communication, we can achieve positive outcomes and foster genuine connection and understanding with others.

II. EFFECTIVE COMMUNICATION TECHNIQUES

Effective communication is key to successfully persuading others and influencing them ethically. There are several techniques that can be employed to enhance one's communication skills and achieve the desired outcome. Firstly, active listening is fundamental to effective communication. This involves giving full attention to the speaker, maintaining eye contact, and avoiding any distractions. By truly hearing and understanding what the other person is saying, it becomes easier to respond appropriately and address their concerns. Another important technique is the use of non-verbal communication cues. These include facial expressions, body language, and gestures, which can greatly impact the message being conveyed. Utilizing appropriate non-verbal cues can enhance the clarity and impact of one's communication, making it more persuasive and influential. Being mindful of one's tone of voice is crucial in communicating effectively. The tone can convey emotions, intentions, and attitudes towards the listener. By adopting a sincere and respectful tone, the speaker can establish rapport and create a positive atmosphere for communication to take place. Being aware of cultural differences and adapting one's communication style accordingly is essential in effectively persuading individuals from diverse backgrounds. Understanding and respecting cultural nuances can help build trust and avoid misunderstandings that may hinder effective communication. Employing storytelling techniques can be a powerful means of persuasion. Humans are naturally drawn to narratives and storytelling allows for the emotional connection necessary to influence others. By presenting information in the form of a story, the listener's attention is captivated, and they are more likely to remember and be persuaded by the message. Another effective technique is using evidence and data to support arguments. Facts and statistics can provide credibility and enhance the persuasiveness of one's communication. By presenting reliable evidence, the speaker can establish themselves as an authority on the subject matter, increasing their chances of influencing others. Ensuring clarity and simplicity in communication is crucial. Using jargon or complex vocabulary may alienate the listener and make the message incomprehensible. It is important to convey ideas in a clear and concise manner, using language that is accessible to the audience. The use of visual aids such as charts, graphs, or slides can greatly enhance the effectiveness of communication. Visuals can simplify complex information, making it easier to understand and remember. They can also serve as a visual representation of the speaker's argument and make it more compelling. Finally, it is important to be empathetic and considerate when communicating with others. Showing genuine care for their needs and perspectives can foster trust and open the door for meaningful dialogue. By acknowledging and understanding the emotions and concerns of the listener, the speaker can tailor their communication to address these concerns effectively. Effective communication techniques are crucial in persuading others ethically. By employing active listening, utilizing non-verbal cues, being mindful of one's tone of voice, adapting to cultural differences, using storytelling techniques, providing evidence, ensuring clarity and simplicity, utilizing visual aids, and being empathetic,

individuals can enhance their communication skills and successfully influence others in various contexts.

A. ACTIVE LISTENING

Active listening is a crucial skill for effective communication and persuasion. It involves carefully and attentively paying attention to what the speaker is saying, both verbally and non-verbally. Active listening requires concentration and a genuine interest in understanding the speaker's perspective. By actively listening, we can gather valuable information, gain insights into the speaker's thoughts and emotions, and develop a deeper connection with them. Active listening involves various techniques such as paraphrasing, summarizing, and reflecting on the speaker's message. One important aspect of active listening is being fully present and giving the speaker our undivided attention. In today's fast-paced and technology-driven world, it is easy to get distracted by various stimuli. By actively listening, we show respect and demonstrate that we value the speaker's thoughts and opinions. Active listening requires us to put aside our own thoughts and biases and focus solely on the speaker's message.

Paraphrasing is another technique that can enhance active listening. It involves restating the speaker's message in our own words to ensure understanding. Paraphrasing allows us to clarify any misunderstandings and demonstrates that we are actively engaged in the conversation. By paraphrasing, we can also confirm our understanding and provide the speaker with an opportunity to clarify or expand on their ideas.

Summarizing is closely related to paraphrasing but involves condensing the main points of the speaker's message. It helps us to remember and retain the key information and provides a concise overview of the discussion. Summarizing also allows us to check our understanding and ensures that we have accurately captured the essence of the speaker's message.

Reflection is another crucial aspect of active listening. It involves expressing our understanding of the speaker's emotions and experiences. Reflection shows empathy and helps to build rapport with the speaker. By reflecting on the speaker's message, we demonstrate that we are listening not only to their words but also to their feelings and experiences. This can foster trust and create a safe space for open and honest communication.

In addition to these techniques, non-verbal cues play an important role in active listening. Non-verbal cues such as maintaining eye contact, nodding, and using appropriate facial expressions can convey our interest and attentiveness to the speaker. These non-verbal cues can also signal our understanding and encourage the speaker to continue sharing their thoughts and feelings. Active listening is not only important in one-on-one conversations but also in group settings. In group discussions, active listening allows us to consider multiple perspectives and build consensus. It helps us to avoid misunderstandings, conflicts, and promotes effective collaboration. By actively listening to each member of the group, we can create a supportive environment that encourages participation and fosters the sharing of diverse ideas. Active listening is essential in professional settings such as leadership roles. Leaders who actively listen to their team members can gain valuable insights, address concerns, and build trust and rapport. Active listening can also enhance problem-solving skills by enabling leaders to gather relevant information, identify underlying issues, and make informed decisions.

Active listening is not without its challenges. It requires patience, self-awareness, and the ability to manage distractions. Cultural and language differences can affect active listening and understanding. It is crucial to be mindful of these differences and adapt our listening techniques accordingly.

Active listening is a vital skill in effective communication and persuasion. By giving our full attention, using techniques such as paraphrasing, summarizing, and reflection, and being aware of non-verbal cues, we can foster meaningful connections, understand different perspectives, and build trust. Active listening is not only important in one-on-one conversations but also in group settings and professional environments. Developing active listening skills can enhance our ability to influence others ethically and create positive and productive relationships.

IMPORTANCE OF ATTENTIVE LISTENING TO UNDERSTAND OTHERS' PERSPECTIVES

Attentive listening plays a crucial role in understanding others' perspectives and is instrumental in effective communication and persuasion. In today's fast-paced world, where information is readily accessible and conversations are often fragmented, we often find ourselves lacking the necessary patience and focus to truly listen to others. The importance of attentive listening cannot be overstated, especially when it comes to influencing others ethically. By attentively listening, we demonstrate respect and empathy towards the speaker, creating a conducive environment for open dialogue and mutual understanding.

Attentive listening not only helps in grasping the speaker's message accurately but also allows us to identify their underlying motivations, emotions, and values, which are key factors in persuasion. When we attentively listen, it means dedicating our full attention to the speaker without interruptions or distractions. This level of focus facilitates the assimilation of information, enables us to pick up on non-verbal cues, and allows us to delve deeper into the speaker's perspective. In doing so, we gain a comprehensive understanding of their thoughts, beliefs, and experiences, all of which are essential in constructing a persuasive argument tailored to their needs and interests. Attentive listening requires us to suspend judgment, set aside our own preconceived notions, and genuinely engage with the speaker's ideas. By doing this, we create a safe space where individuals feel heard and respected, fostering trust and openness in the process.

Attentive listening goes beyond comprehending the speaker's words; it involves actively engaging with their emotions and non-verbal cues. People often communicate not only through their words but also through their tone, facial expressions, and body language. Attentive listeners are sensitive to these subtleties, allowing them not only to understand the speaker's literal message but also to interpret the underlying emotions and intentions. This holistic approach to listening enables us to connect with others on a deeper level, empathize with their concerns, and acknowledge their perspectives even if they differ from our own. It is through this empathetic connection that we find common ground and build bridges of understanding, making persuasive communication more effective and authentic.

Attentive listening also helps us uncover the motivations behind others' perspectives. Every individual has their unique set of values, beliefs, and experiences that shape their worldview. By actively listening, we become attuned to these underlying factors, enabling us to engage with the speaker's motivations.

Understanding these motivations is pivotal in constructing persuasive arguments that resonate with the speaker's desires and interests. By aligning our message with their values and aspirations, we can present a compelling case that appeals to their rationality and emotional needs simultaneously. Attentive listening also allows us to identify any potential barriers to persuasion. By grasping the speaker's anxieties, concerns, or reservations, we can tailor our argument to address these factors and alleviate their worries. This personalized approach increases the likelihood of successful persuasion, as it acknowledges and respects the individuality of the listener. In addition to aiding persuasion, attentive listening also promotes effective communication by creating an atmosphere of trust and authenticity. In our increasingly fractured society, where conflicting opinions and ideologies dominate public discourse, active listening enables us to find common ground and foster meaningful dialogue. It encourages individuals to share their perspectives openly and honestly, knowing that they will be genuinely heard and respected. By actively demonstrating our interest in the speaker's thoughts and feelings, we establish a rapport built on trust and mutual understanding. This fosters constructive conversations where disagreements can be addressed respectfully, and different viewpoints can be explored collaboratively. Attentive listening is, therefore, an essential tool in navigating diverse social, cultural, and political contexts, promoting inclusivity, and expanding our horizons.

To conclude, attentive listening plays a crucial role in understanding others' perspectives and is essential for effective communication and persuasion. Through attentive listening, we demonstrate respect, empathy, and understanding towards the speaker, fostering an environment conducive to open dialogue and mutual understanding. It enables us to grasp the speaker's message accurately, identify their motivations and values, and engage with their emotions and non-verbal cues. Attentive listening allows us to construct persuasive arguments that resonate with the listener's desires and interests, tailored to address any potential barriers to persuasion. By actively listening, we create an atmosphere of trust and authenticity, promoting constructive conversations and bridging gaps in diverse contexts. In a world where effective communication is invaluable, attentive listening stands out as a powerful tool for understanding others and influencing them ethically.

DEMONSTRATING RESPECT AND EMPATHY THROUGH VERBAL AND NON-VERBAL CUES

Demonstrating respect and empathy through verbal and non-verbal cues is essential in effective communication and persuasion. Respect is the foundation of any healthy relationship, and it should be the cornerstone of persuasive communication as well. When interacting with others, whether in a personal or professional setting, it is important to convey respect through both verbal and non-verbal cues. Verbal cues that demonstrate respect include using polite language, addressing the other person by their preferred name or title, and actively listening to their thoughts and opinions. By using phrases such as "please" and "thank you," we show appreciation for the other person's time and input. Using inclusive and non-discriminatory language and avoiding offensive jokes or remarks is crucial in conveying respect and empathy. In addition to verbal cues, non-verbal cues play a significant role in demonstrating respect and empathy. Body language, facial expressions, and eye contact are all non-verbal cues that can convey respect and empathy. When engaged in conversation with someone, maintaining open body language, such as keeping arms uncrossed and facing the person, signals that we are interested and attentive. Making eye contact shows that we are actively listening and value what the other person has to say. By nodding and using affirming gestures, we can help the other person feel heard and validated.

A central component of demonstrating empathy is being aware of and sensitive to the other person's emotions. Empathy involves understanding and sharing another person's feelings, and this can be achieved through both verbal and non-verbal cues. One effective verbal cue to show empathy is to use reflective listening techniques. Reflective listening involves paraphrasing the other person's statements to ensure understanding and validate their feelings. For example, if someone expresses frustration, we can respond by saying, "I understand that this situation is causing you frustration, and I can see why." This shows that we are acknowledging and empathizing with their emotions.

Non-verbal cues that demonstrate empathy include mirroring the other person's body language and facial expressions. This helps create a sense of rapport and shows that we are attuned to their emotional state. Using a calm and soothing tone of voice can convey empathy and reassurance. By being aware of these non-verbal cues, we can create an environment where the other person feels understood and supported.

It is important to note that demonstrating respect and empathy through verbal and non-verbal cues should be done genuinely and authentically. People are perceptive and can quickly detect insincerity or manipulation. It is crucial to approach persuasion with genuine respect for the other person's perspective and a sincere desire to understand their needs and emotions. Authenticity is key to building trust and fostering a positive relationship.

The power dynamic between the persuader and the audience should be considered when demonstrating respect and empathy. In some cases, the persuader may hold a higher rank or authority than the audience. It is essential in these situations to be mindful of potential power imbalances and avoid patronizing or condescending language. Treating the audience as equals and valuing their input is crucial in building trust and creating a persuasive message that resonates with them.

Demonstrating respect and empathy through verbal and non-verbal cues is essential in effective communication and persuasion. Respect can be conveyed through polite language, active listening, and inclusive communication, while empathy can be demonstrated through reflective listening, mirroring body language, and using a calm tone of voice. It is important to approach persuasion with authenticity and genuine respect for the other person's perspective. By considering the power dynamics and treating the audience as equals, we can build trust and create a persuasive message that effectively influences others ethically.

USING CLARIFYING QUESTIONS TO ENSURE A CLEAR UNDERSTANDING OF THE OTHER PERSON'S VIEWPOINT

In addition to active listening, using clarifying questions is another effective strategy to ensure a clear understanding of the other person's viewpoint. Clarifying questions are questions that seek to clarify specific points or aspects of the other person's perspective. They help to fill in the gaps and remove any ambiguities or assumptions that may exist. By asking clarifying questions, a person can demonstrate genuine interest in understanding the other person's viewpoint and also gather more information to make an informed response. One way that clarifying questions can be used is by seeking further information or examples. For example, if someone states an opinion or belief that we are not familiar with, we can ask them to provide specific examples or evidence to support their viewpoint. By doing so, we can gain a deeper understanding of the reasoning behind their perspective and evaluate it more objectively. This can also help to uncover any underlying assumptions or biases that may be influencing their viewpoint. Another way clarifying questions can be used is by seeking to understand the underlying motivations or values that drive the other person's viewpoint. For example, if someone expresses a strong opinion on an issue, we can ask them why they feel that way or what values they believe are at stake. By understanding the deeper motivations or values behind their viewpoint, we can better appreciate their perspective and find common ground or points of agreement. Clarifying questions can also be used to identify any areas of misunderstanding or confusion. Sometimes, when engaging in a discussion or debate, it is possible for miscommunication to occur. By asking clarifying questions, we can ensure that we are on the same page and avoid any unnecessary conflicts or misunderstandings. For example, if someone makes a statement that seems contradictory or unclear, we can ask for clarification to ensure that we are interpreting their words correctly. Asking clarifying questions can also help to challenge and expand our own thinking. When we engage with others who have different viewpoints, it can be tempting to dismiss or ignore their perspectives. By asking clarifying questions, we can challenge our own assumptions and broaden our understanding of the issue at hand. This can lead to more informed and nuanced discussions, as we become more open to considering alternative perspectives and ideas. It is important to approach asking clarifying questions with a genuine intention to understand, rather than to interrogate or invalidate the other person's viewpoint. The tone and phrasing of the questions we ask can greatly impact how the other person perceives our intentions. By asking open-ended questions and using a non-confrontational tone, we can create a safe and open environment for dialogue, minimizing defensiveness and promoting a more constructive conversation. The use of clarifying questions is a valuable tool in ensuring a clear understanding of the other person's viewpoint. By seeking further information, understanding underlying motivations, identifying areas of confusion, and challenging our own thinking, clarifying questions can enhance our ability to communicate effectively and persuasively with others. When used ethically and sincerely, these questions can promote understanding, bridge differences, and foster meaningful conversations. In an increasingly polarized world, the art of using clarifying questions is an essential skill to cultivate for productive and respectful communication.

B. BUILDING CREDIBILITY

Building credibility is an essential aspect of effective persuasion. Credibility refers to the trustworthiness and expertise that individuals attribute to a speaker or message. Without credibility, it becomes challenging to influence others ethically. Several strategies can be employed to enhance credibility. Firstly, it is crucial to establish oneself as an expert in the field. By demonstrating extensive knowledge and expertise, individuals are more likely to view the speaker as credible and reliable. This can be achieved through providing evidence, citing credible sources, and presenting logical arguments that are well-grounded in the relevant body of knowledge. Speakers should strive to maintain consistency in their message and behavior. Inconsistency can undermine credibility, as it gives the impression of dishonesty or instability. It is important to align one's words with their actions, consistently deliver the intended message, and follow through on promises made. Incorporating storytelling and personal experiences can contribute to building credibility. Sharing personal anecdotes or experiences that relate to the topic at hand helps to establish authenticity and shows that the speaker has firsthand knowledge or understanding of the subject matter. This can create a sense of relatability and trust with the audience. The use of non-verbal cues can significantly impact credibility. Maintaining proper eye contact, delivering speeches with confidence, and using appropriate body language can enhance credibility as they indicate sincerity and conviction. Any signs of nervousness or uncertainty can weaken the perception of credibility. It is important to consider the context in which persuasion is taking place. Tailoring one's message to align with the values, beliefs, and needs of the audience can greatly enhance credibility. By demonstrating an understanding of the audience's perspective and concerns, the speaker shows that they are genuinely interested in their well-being and their needs. Building credibility also involves recognizing and acknowledging any potential biases or conflicts of interest. Failure to do so can lead to a loss of credibility as it appears dishonest or self-serving. By being transparent about any potential biases or conflicts, the speaker demonstrates integrity and enhances their credibility by allowing the audience to make informed decisions. Building credibility is a crucial component of persuasion. By establishing oneself as an expert, maintaining consistency, incorporating personal experiences, utilizing non-verbal cues, adapting to the audience's needs, and acknowledging biases, individuals can enhance their credibility and effectively influence others ethically.

ESTABLISHING EXPERTISE THROUGH KNOWLEDGE AND EXPERIENCE

Establishing expertise through knowledge and experience is a crucial aspect of the art of persuasion. To effectively influence others, individuals must first have a solid foundation of knowledge in the subject matter at hand. This knowledge can be gained through a variety of means, such as formal education, extensive research, and hands-on experience. When someone demonstrates their expertise, it not only enhances their credibility but also allows them to present their ideas and arguments with confidence and clarity. This is particularly important in academic and professional contexts where expertise plays a key role in influencing decision-making processes. For instance, in a research conference, a presenter who has conducted thorough investigations and possesses a deep understanding of the topic is more likely to be persuasive than someone who lacks expertise. Having experience in the field further strengthens one's ability to persuade others. Practical knowledge acquired through years of experience can greatly enrich the persuasive process by providing real-world examples, insights, and solutions. This combination of knowledge and experience serves to establish credibility and demonstrates to the audience that the persuader is not only well-informed but also has practical know-how. The persuasive power of expertise can be seen in various fields, from medicine to politics. In the medical field, doctors who are experts in their respective specialties can easily sway their patients to follow their recommendations due to their extensive knowledge and experience.

Similarly, politicians who have demonstrated expertise in a particular policy area are often more successful in garnering public support for their proposals. By effectively leveraging their expertise, these individuals are able to make compelling arguments that resonate with their target audience. It is important to note that expertise alone is not enough to persuade others ethically. It must be combined with effective communication strategies that take into account the needs, values, and beliefs of the audience. Persuasion is not about manipulation or coercion but rather about presenting information in a compelling manner that appeals to the rational and emotional sides of individuals. To achieve this, the persuader must understand the mindset of their audience and tailor their message accordingly. By doing so, they can establish a connection with their audience and build trust, which in turn enhances their persuasive power. Using ethical persuasion techniques that promote transparency, honesty, and respect for the autonomy of others is essential. Ethical persuasion recognizes the rights and agency of individuals, allowing them to make informed decisions based on accurate information rather than being coerced into accepting a particular viewpoint. By focusing on establishing expertise through knowledge and experience and applying ethical persuasion techniques, individuals can effectively influence others while maintaining respect for their autonomy. Establishing expertise through knowledge and experience is a vital component of persuasive communication. The combination of in-depth knowledge and practical experience enhances credibility, allowing individuals to present their ideas and arguments with confidence and clarity. Expertise alone is not sufficient; it must be coupled with effective communication strategies that consider the needs, values, and beliefs of the audience. By understanding the mindset of the audience, tailoring messages accordingly, and employing ethical persuasion techniques, individuals can influence others ethically while promoting transparency and respecting autonomy. The art of persuasion lies in finding the balance between presenting information convincingly and maintaining the ethical principles of persuasive communication.

HIGHLIGHTING SHARED VALUES OR COMMON GROUND

In addition to understanding the importance of building credibility and using persuasive strategies, it is crucial to highlight shared values and common ground when attempting to influence others ethically. When individuals perceive similarities or shared values between themselves and the persuader, they are more likely to be receptive to the message being conveyed. This is because people tend to trust others who they perceive as similar to themselves, as this similarity fosters a sense of connection and understanding. By emphasizing shared values and finding common ground with the audience, the persuader can establish a sense of trust and increase the likelihood of the desired outcome.

One way to highlight shared values is to appeal to the audience's sense of identity. Humans have a strong need for identity and belonging, and aligning oneself with certain values and beliefs forms part of one's self-concept. By connecting the message to the audience's sense of self, the persuader can tap into their identity and establish a common ground. For example, if the persuader is advocating for environmental conservation, they can emphasize how protecting the environment aligns with the audience's value of being responsible citizens. Framing the message in a way that resonates with the audience's identity creates a sense of unity and fosters a positive perception of the persuader's motives. Another strategy to highlight shared values is to appeal to the audience's sense of community. Humans are social creatures, and we often find comfort and security in belonging to groups. By highlighting the shared values within a community, the persuader can leverage the power of social influence. For instance, if the intended audience is a group of teachers, the persuader can emphasize how the proposed idea or action aligns with the goals and values of the teaching community. This appeals to the audience's desire to conform to the norms of their community and fosters a sense of unity. By positioning the message as a collective effort, the persuader reinforces the idea that the desired outcome benefits not just the individual, but the entire community as well. Cultivating a sense of empathy is another effective way to highlight shared values and common ground. Empathy involves understanding and sharing the feelings and perspectives of others. By demonstrating empathy towards the audience's concerns, the persuader can establish a connection and create a mutual understanding. For instance, if the persuader is advocating for better healthcare policies, they can share personal stories or experiences that demonstrate empathy towards the difficulties and challenges faced by individuals in accessing healthcare services. This can evoke emotions in the audience and create a sense of shared understanding, making them more receptive to the persuader's message. Finding common ground through shared experiences can be a powerful way to highlight shared values. Humans tend to bond over shared experiences, as they foster a sense of unity and connectedness. By referencing common experiences or situations, the persuader can establish a rapport with the audience and build trust. For example, if the persuader is trying to promote the importance of mental health awareness, they could begin by referencing the common struggles and stresses of everyday life that everyone can relate to. This allows the audience to see themselves in the message and increases the likelihood that they will be open to the persuader's suggestions. It is important to note that highlighting shared values and common ground does not mean compromising one's own beliefs or values. Instead, it is about finding areas in which both parties can agree or relate to, while still staying true to the persuader's objectives. By identifying shared values, the persuader can bridge the gap between themselves and the audience, creating an environment conducive to effective communication and ethical influence. Highlighting shared values and common ground is an essential aspect of ethical persuasion. By appealing to the audience's sense of identity, community, empathy, and shared experiences, the persuader can establish trust and create a connection with the audience. This connection fosters a positive perception of the persuader's motives and increases the likelihood of the desired outcome. Understanding the psychology of persuasion and effective communication, alongside the importance of building credibility and utilizing persuasive strategies, is crucial for individuals seeking to ethically influence others in various contexts.

PRESENTING ONESELF AS TRUSTWORTHY AND RELIABLE

In order to successfully persuade others, it is crucial to present oneself as trustworthy and reliable. Trustworthiness is the foundation of any effective communication, as it establishes credibility and fosters a sense of reliability. When individuals perceive someone as trustworthy, they are more likely to be open to their ideas and opinions. Trust can be built through various means, such as demonstrating competence, displaying transparency, and keeping one's promises. Competence is essential as it helps establish credibility and expertise in a given domain. When individuals perceive someone as competent, they are more inclined to listen to and value their input. Demonstrating transparency is another important aspect of establishing trustworthiness. By being open and honest about one's intentions, motives, and limitations, individuals can create an atmosphere of trust and reliability. It is crucial to keep one's promises. Following through on commitments not only demonstrates reliability but also builds trust over time. When people see that someone consistently acts in accordance with their words, they are more likely to view them as trustworthy. Reliability is closely tied to trustworthiness, as it entails consistent and dependable behavior. Being reliable means doing what one says they will do and being consistent in their actions. When individuals perceive someone as reliable, they are more likely to trust and rely on them in return. Reliability can be demonstrated through punctuality, consistency in actions, and being accountable for one's commitments. Punctuality is particularly significant, as it reflects an individual's respect for others' time and their own responsibilities. Consistency in actions, on the other hand, shows predictability and dependability, which are key factors in building trust and reliability. Being accountable for one's commitments is crucial in establishing oneself as reliable. Taking responsibility for one's actions, acknowledging mistakes, and working towards rectification demonstrates integrity and reliability. Establishing trustworthiness and reliability is vital not only in personal relationships but also in various professional and social contexts. In the workplace, for instance, leaders and managers who are perceived as trustworthy and reliable are better able to influence their team members and inspire trust and loyalty. Employees are more likely to follow a leader who is competent, transparent, and consistent in their actions. By creating an environment of trust and reliability, leaders can foster better cooperation, collaboration, and productivity among their team members. Trustworthiness and reliability are also crucial in marketing and advertising. Consumers are more likely to buy products or services from a brand they trust and perceive as reliable. Trustworthy brands are seen as more credible, and consumers are more willing to engage with them, recommend them to others, and become loyal customers. One of the keyways to establish trustworthiness and reliability in marketing is through providing accurate information, being transparent about product or service features, and consistently delivering on promises. Similarly, in interpersonal relationships, trustworthiness and reliability form the basis for healthy and fulfilling connections. When individuals trust each other and can rely on one another, it creates a sense of security, intimacy, and support. Trustworthy and reliable friends are more likely to be confided in, sought for advice, and relied upon during times of need. Presenting oneself as trustworthy and reliable is indispensable for effective persuasion and communication. Trustworthiness and reliability are built through demonstrating competence, displaying transparency, and keeping one's promises. Competence establishes credibility and expertise, while transparency creates an atmosphere of trust and reliability. Keeping one's promises and consistently following through on commitments demonstrates dependability. Establishing trustworthiness and reliability is not only important in personal relationships but also in professional and social contexts, such as the workplace and marketing. Trustworthy and reliable leaders are better equipped to influence and inspire their team members, while trustworthy brands are more appealing to consumers. Trustworthiness and reliability contribute to healthy and fulfilling interpersonal connections.

C. EMOTIONAL APPEAL

Emotional appeal, also known as pathos, is a persuasive technique that relies on evoking emotions in the audience to influence their thoughts, beliefs, and behaviors. This approach is grounded in the understanding that humans are inherently emotional beings, and our emotions play a significant role in decision-making processes. By tapping into and manipulating these emotions, persuasive communicators can sway an audience's opinions and actions. Emotional appeal can be particularly effective when combined with logical reasoning and credibility building, as it adds an extra layer of relatability and connection between the message sender and the recipients. It is important to note that emotional appeal can be a double-edged sword, as it can be used unethically to exploit vulnerable individuals or promote harmful agendas. One of the key aspects of emotional appeal is identifying and understanding the emotions that are most likely to resonate with the target audience. Different people have different emotional triggers, and what may stir one person's emotions may have no impact on another. Persuasive communicators must undertake careful research and analysis to identify the emotions that are most relevant and compelling to their target audience. This can be done through surveys, focus groups, or by drawing upon existing psychological research on emotions and persuasion. By tailoring their message to address these specific emotions, communicators can increase the effectiveness of their appeals. In order to elicit emotional responses, persuasive communicators employ a variety of techniques. One common tactic is storytelling, which involves presenting real or hypothetical narratives that evoke empathy, compassion, or sympathy. By sharing personal anecdotes or relatable stories, communicators can humanize complex issues and make them more emotionally engaging. For example, a nonprofit organization advocating for animal rights might tell the story of a mistreated dog to elicit feelings of empathy and compassion, motivating the audience to take action against animal cruelty. Another strategy is the use of vivid imagery, which involves painting a detailed and emotionally charged mental picture in the minds of the audience. This can be accomplished through descriptive language, metaphors, or even visual aids such as photographs or videos. By appealing to the audience's senses, communicators can evoke powerful emotions and make their message more memorable and impactful.

In addition to storytelling and vivid imagery, persuasive communicators can also leverage other emotional triggers such as fear, anger, happiness, or nostalgia. Fear appeal, for instance, can be used to highlight the negative consequences of not following a desired course of action. By emphasizing the potential risks or dangers, communicators can tap into the audience's fear and motivate them to take preventive measures. It is crucial to strike a balance between creating fear and providing realistic solutions, as excessive fear may lead to a feeling of helplessness and disengagement. Similarly, anger appeal can be employed to channel the audience's anger towards a particular issue or individual, inspiring them to take a stand or support a specific cause. It is important to ensure that the anger is directed towards the issue at hand and not misdirected towards innocent parties.

While emotional appeal can be a powerful tool for persuasion, it is essential to use it ethically and responsibly. Manipulating people's emotions for personal gain or to advance harmful agendas is not only unethical but can also undermine trust and credibility. Persuasive communicators should strive to be transparent, honest, and respectful of their audience's autonomy. They should provide accurate information, avoid misleading or exaggerated claims, and allow individuals to make informed decisions based on a balance of both emotional and rational considerations. It is important to recognize that emotional appeal is not a one-size-fits-all approach and that different cultures, personalities, and contexts may require tailored strategies. Sensitivity to cultural norms and individual differences can enhance the effectiveness of emotional appeals and promote ethical persuasion.

Emotional appeal is a persuasive technique that harnesses the power of emotions to influence an audience's thoughts, beliefs, and behaviors. By evoking emotions such as empathy, compassion, fear, anger, or nostalgia, communicators can make their message more relatable, engaging, and memorable. It is important to use emotional appeal ethically and responsibly, avoiding manipulation and respecting the autonomy of the audience. Through careful research, thoughtful storytelling, and a balance of emotional and logical appeals, persuasive communicators can leverage emotional appeal to ethically influence others.

THE ROLE OF EMOTIONS IN DECISION-MAKING

Understanding the role of emotions in decision-making is crucial in the field of psychology and has been the subject of extensive research. Emotions play a significant role in shaping our decision-making processes as they have the ability to exert a powerful influence on our thoughts, behaviors, and judgment. Traditionally, decision-making was thought to be a rational and logical process based solely on cognitive factors. Recent theories and empirical findings have challenged this view by highlighting the intricate relationship between emotions and decision-making. Emotions are complex psychological experiences that involve physiological arousal, subjective feelings, and behavioral expressions. These experiences are typically triggered by external events or internal thoughts, and they can vary in intensity, valence, and duration. The role of emotions in decision-making can be best understood through two prominent theories: the Somatic Marker Theory and the Dual Process Theory. The Somatic Marker Theory, proposed by Antonio Damasio, suggests that emotions serve as crucial cognitive resources that guide our decision-making. According to this theory, emotions are responsible for creating markers or tags that are associated with specific experiences or situations. When faced with a decision, these somatic markers are activated and influence our choices by providing quick, intuitive, and affective responses. For instance, if an individual has a negative emotional experience associated with a particular course of action, such as losing money in the past, this negative emotion acts as a somatic marker that signals caution and discourages them from making a similar choice in the future. On the other hand, positive emotional experiences can serve as markers that promote exploration and encourage individuals to take certain risks. This theory suggests that emotions enable us to make advantageous decisions by integrating past experiences into our decision-making process and ultimately guiding us toward favorable outcomes.

The Dual Process Theory provides another perspective on the role of emotions in decision-making. According to this theory, decision-making relies on two distinct processes: the intuitive system and the analytical system. The intuitive system, fuelled by emotions, operates rapidly and automatically, enabling individuals to make quick decisions based on instinct and gut feelings. In contrast, the analytical system, driven by cognitive deliberation and logical reasoning, takes longer to generate an outcome.

While the intuitive system is dominated by emotions, the analytical system is more rational and objective in its approach. The Dual Process Theory suggests that both systems interact and work together in decision-making, with the intuitive system often serving as the primary driver of choices. Emotions serve as a valuable tool in this process by providing rapid evaluations of the available options, thereby steering individuals towards decision outcomes that are consistent with their emotional states.

Many studies have provided empirical evidence to support the role of emotions in decision-making. For example, Bechara et al. (1997) conducted a study on individuals with brain damage in the ventromedial prefrontal cortex, a region associated with emotional processing. They found that these individuals were impaired in making advantageous decisions in a gambling task. This impairment was attributed to the absence of emotional signals, suggesting that emotions play a critical role in guiding decision-making toward favorable outcomes. Similarly, researchers have demonstrated the impact of emotions on decision-making in domains such as consumer behavior, financial choices, and risk-taking. These findings highlight the pervasive influence of emotions on our decision-making processes and emphasize the need for a comprehensive understanding of their role.

In addition to influencing individual decision-making, emotions also play a crucial role in persuasive communication and the art of persuasion. Persuasion is an essential social skill that involves influencing others' attitudes, beliefs, and behaviors. Emotions are effective tools in persuasion as they can elicit powerful emotional responses in the target audience, which in turn can shape their decision-making process. For instance, advertisers often use emotional appeals in their advertisements to evoke positive emotions and establish a connection between the product or service and positive experiences. This emotional connection can influence the consumer's decision-making by creating a desire for the product or service and increasing the chances of purchase or adoption of the desired behavior. Emotions also serve as important factors in ethical persuasion. Ethical persuasion involves maintaining transparency, respecting others' autonomy, and ensuring informed consent. Emotions can be used ethically in persuasion if they are employed with the intent of fostering understanding and empathy rather than manipulation or coercion. By appealing to people's emotions, ethical communicators can create a sense of shared values, empathy, and trust, allowing them to influence others in a positive and constructive manner. It is crucial to note that ethical persuasion should always prioritize the well-being and autonomy of individuals, ensuring that their emotions are not exploited or manipulated for personal gain.

Understanding the role of emotions in decision-making is crucial in various contexts, including psychology, consumer behavior, risk-taking, and persuasive communication. Emotions shape our decision-making processes by providing intuitive responses, creating markers associated with specific experiences, and influencing our choices through rapid evaluations. The Somatic Marker Theory and the Dual Process Theory provide valuable insights into the complex interplay between emotions and decision-making. Emotions play a significant role in persuasive communication, allowing individuals to influence others' attitudes and behaviors ethically. Appreciating the role of emotions in decision-making can enhance our decision-making skills, facilitate effective communication, and ultimately contribute to successful outcomes in different areas of life.

ELICITING EMOTIONS THROUGH STORYTELLING AND PERSONAL ANECDOTES

Storytelling has long been recognized as a powerful tool for eliciting emotions and connecting with an audience on a deep level. The use of personal anecdotes enhances this emotional connection, as it brings the storyteller's experiences and emotions into the narrative. When individuals share personal stories, they are essentially opening up a window into their own lives, allowing the audience to relate to their experiences and feel a sense of empathy. This emotional connection not only captivates the audience's attention but also allows the storyteller to influence their thoughts and beliefs. By sharing personal anecdotes, speakers and writers can effectively tap into the emotions of their audience, leading them to experience a range of feelings, such as joy, sadness, nostalgia, or even anger. These emotions, in turn, can shape the audience's perception of the message being conveyed and influence their decision-making process. For example, a public speaker discussing the importance of environmental conservation may recount a personal story of witnessing the devastating effects of pollution on a once pristine landscape. This story could evoke feelings of sadness and concern in the audience, prompting them to become more receptive to the speaker's call to action. Similarly, a writer addressing the issue of social injustice may share a personal anecdote about an experience with discrimination, evoking anger and empathy in the readers, and motivating them to take a stand against injustice. In both cases, the storyteller's use of personal anecdotes effectively elicits emotions that align with their intended message, thus increasing their persuasive influence. Storytelling and personal anecdotes can also facilitate the creation of memorable and relatable narratives. When information is presented in the form of a story, it becomes more engaging and easier to remember. This is because stories have a naturally cohesive structure that allows the audience to follow along and make connections between different elements of the narrative. By incorporating personal anecdotes, the storyteller adds a unique and personal touch to the story, making it even more memorable. This is because personal anecdotes are often imbued with vivid details and specific emotions that resonate with the audience. For instance, a storyteller sharing a personal anecdote about a childhood pet may describe the pet's physical appearance, personality traits, and the emotions they experienced upon losing it. This rich and detailed narrative creates a lasting impression in the audience's minds, allowing them to recall the story and its underlying message long after they have heard or read it. Personal anecdotes make stories more relatable by connecting the audience to the storyteller's personal experiences. When individuals hear or read about someone else's experiences, they often form connections with their own lives, drawing parallels between the two. This sense of connection helps the audience to better understand and internalize the message being conveyed. If a speaker discussing the challenges of overcoming adversity shares a personal anecdote about their own struggles, the audience members who have faced similar challenges can relate to their story and feel a sense of validation. This relatability allows the audience to connect emotionally with the speaker and be more receptive to their message. One can see how impactful storytelling and personal anecdotes can be in persuading others and influencing their thoughts and actions. It is important to note that the use of such tools should always be ethical and considerate of the audience's emotions. Persuasive storytelling should never manipulate the audience's emotions or exploit vulnerable individuals. Instead, it should aim to foster genuine empathy and understanding, encouraging the audience to reflect on their own beliefs and values. Storytelling and personal anecdotes have the power to elicit emotions, create memorable narratives, and establish relatability with the audience. By incorporating personal experiences into their stories, speakers and writers can effectively connect with their audience on an emotional level, leading to a greater persuasive impact. It is of utmost importance that these tools are used ethically and responsibly, always taking into consideration the emotions and well-being of the audience. When used effectively and ethically, storytelling and personal anecdotes can become powerful tools for influencing others in various contexts.

EMPATHY AND GENUINE CONCERN TO CREATE A MEANINGFUL CONNECTION

In the realm of persuasion and effective communication, one cannot overlook the significance of empathy and genuine concern as crucial elements in creating a meaningful connection with others. Empathy, defined as the ability to understand and share the feelings of another, plays a pivotal role in establishing rapport, fostering trust, and ultimately influencing others. When individuals perceive that someone genuinely cares about their thoughts, emotions, and needs, they are more likely to be receptive to and persuaded by that person's message or request. This is because empathy creates a sense of validation and recognition, affirming individuals' worth and importance, and signaling that their perspectives are valued. Effective communicators understand this fundamental aspect of human psychology and seek to cultivate empathy as a core part of their persuasive strategy. They immerse themselves in other individuals' experiences, seeking to grasp not only the external circumstances but also the nuanced emotions and motivations that underlie their perspectives. By doing so, communicators can connect on a deeper level with their target audience, enabling them to tailor their messages in ways that resonate with individuals' specific concerns and aspirations. For instance, a salesperson aiming to convince a potential customer to purchase a product may employ empathy by first understanding the customer's personal needs and desires, and then highlighting how the product can address those particular concerns. By demonstrating that they genuinely empathize with the customer's situation, the salesperson establishes a sense of trust, paving the way for a more impactful persuasive interaction.

In addition to empathy, genuine concern further reinforces the creation of a meaningful connection in the realm of persuasion. Genuine concern encompasses a sincere, authentic interest and care for the well-being and success of others. When individuals perceive that someone is genuinely invested in their welfare, they are more likely to be open to engaging in a dialogue or being influenced by that person's arguments. Genuine concern goes beyond mere superficial niceties or attempts to manipulate others for personal gain. It involves actively listening, showing empathy, and taking actions that demonstrate a commitment to addressing the needs and concerns of others. One notable example of how genuine concern can contribute to a meaningful connection and effective persuasion is found in the realm of leadership. Effective leaders are those who demonstrate a sincere concern for the growth and development of their team members. They take the time to understand individuals' aspirations, strengths, and areas for improvement, and provide them with the necessary support, guidance, and resources to enhance their skills and achieve their goals. This genuine concern fosters a sense of loyalty and commitment from team members, as they feel valued and appreciated for their unique contributions. As a result, leaders who prioritize genuine concern are more likely to inspire their teams to go above and beyond, achieving exceptional results and successes. In the context of social and political activism, empathy and genuine concern play a vital role in rallying support and effecting change. Activists who genuinely empathize with the experiences and struggles of marginalized communities are more likely to draw attention to important social issues and catalyze collective action. By shining a light on the lived realities faced by those affected, they create a connection with a broader audience, compelling them to question their own privilege and actively contribute to positive social transformation. Genuine concern sustains this connection, as activists consistently prioritize the well-being and rights of those they seek to empower, ensuring that their efforts are aligned with the agenda and priorities of the communities they serve. Empathy and genuine concern occupy a central position in the realm of persuasion and effective communication. By expressing empathy, communicators validate and acknowledge the experiences of others, fostering trust and receptiveness to their messages. Genuine concern further reinforces this connection, demonstrating a sincere interest in the well-being and success of others. Both empathy and genuine concern work synergistically to establish a meaningful connection, enabling communicators to tailor their messages to individuals' specific concerns and aspirations. Whether in sales, leadership, or social activism, individuals who prioritize empathy and genuine concern are more likely to influence and persuade others ethically, creating a positive impact in diverse contexts.

D. LOGICAL REASONING

Logical reasoning is a vital aspect of effective persuasion and communication, as it provides a basis for establishing the validity of one's arguments and ideas. It involves the process of using rational thinking and valid evidence to arrive at a sound conclusion. In the context of persuasion, logical reasoning allows individuals to present their ideas in a clear and coherent manner, making it easier for others to understand and potentially accept their viewpoints. To engage in logical reasoning effectively, it requires individuals to have a strong grasp of logical fallacies, critical thinking skills, and cognitive biases that may hinder rational decision-making. By utilizing logical reasoning, one can navigate through complex issues, challenge false narratives, and construct compelling arguments that are built on evidence and sound logic.

One of the key components of logical reasoning is identifying and understanding logical fallacies. Logical fallacies are flawed patterns of reasoning that can negatively impact the validity of an argument. These fallacies can take various forms, such as ad hominem attacks, strawman arguments, or appeals to authority. By being able to recognize these fallacies, individuals can evaluate the strength of an argument or statement critically. By challenging faulty reasoning, one can counteract the persuasive tactics employed by others and present a more cogent perspective. Logical reasoning empowers individuals to assess the quality of information they receive and make informed decisions based on sound logic rather than fallacious reasoning.

Critical thinking skills are another essential element of logical reasoning. Critical thinking entails the ability to analyze and evaluate information objectively, without being swayed by personal biases or preconceived notions. This skill allows individuals to engage in thoughtful exploration of ideas, separate facts from opinions, and consider alternative viewpoints. Employing critical thinking enables individuals to assess the credibility of the sources from which they obtain information and evaluate the reasoning behind different arguments. By challenging assumptions and examining evidence, individuals can navigate through complex issues and engage in productive discussions that lead to well-supported conclusions. To engage in logical reasoning, one must also be aware of the cognitive biases that can impair rational decision-making. Cognitive biases are inherent psychological tendencies that can lead individuals to make irrational judgments or to be influenced by their emotions or personal beliefs. For instance, confirmation bias is the tendency to seek or interpret information in a way that confirms one's preexisting beliefs, while the bandwagon effect refers to the tendency to adopt the beliefs or behaviors of a majority. Being conscious of these biases is crucial, as it allows individuals to approach arguments and evidence in a more objective and rational manner. By mitigating the impact of cognitive biases, logical reasoning enables individuals to make decisions based on accurate information and well-founded arguments. When individuals engage in logical reasoning, they can construct persuasive arguments that are built on evidence and sound logic. This process involves presenting a clear and coherent line of reasoning, backed by relevant facts and information. By providing evidence that supports their claims, individuals can establish credibility and encourage others to consider their viewpoints. Logical reasoning allows individuals to anticipate and address counterarguments effectively, strengthening their overall persuasive power. By acknowledging and countering opposing viewpoints, individuals demonstrate a willingness to engage in a fair and balanced discussion, increasing the likelihood that others will be persuaded by their arguments. Logical reasoning plays a crucial role in effective persuasion and communication. By understanding logical fallacies, honing critical thinking skills, and being aware of cognitive biases, individuals can engage in more rational decision-making and construct persuasive arguments. By utilizing logical reasoning, individuals can navigate through complex issues, challenge false narratives, and construct compelling arguments that are built on evidence and sound logic. Logical reasoning empowers individuals to make well-supported decisions and influence others ethically by presenting their ideas in a clear and compelling manner.

STRUCTURING ARGUMENTS WITH CLEAR PREMISES AND CONCLUSIONS

In order to effectively persuade others, it is crucial to structure arguments with clear premises and conclusions. Clear premises ensure that the foundation of an argument is strong and logical, while clear conclusions provide a concise summary of the main points. By structuring arguments in this way, individuals can enhance the persuasiveness of their message and increase the likelihood of others accepting their viewpoint. Clear premises serve as evidence or supporting statements that substantiate the main argument. These premises provide a logical progression of ideas, allowing the audience to follow the reasoning and make informed judgments. For instance, if someone is trying to convince others to support a particular environmental policy, they might present premises such as the negative impact of pollution on public health, the potential benefits of renewable energy, and the success of similar policies in other countries. By presenting these clear premises, the speaker is providing the audience with concrete evidence that strengthens the overall argument. Clear conclusions, on the other hand, help to summarize the key points and leave a lasting impact on the listeners' minds. A strong conclusion should be concise, memorable, and compelling, recapping the main argument and leaving the audience with a clear understanding of the persuasive message. For example, a speaker advocating for a change in education policy might conclude with a powerful statement such as, "By investing in our children's education, we are investing in a brighter future for society as a whole." This conclusion effectively encapsulates the main argument and leaves the audience with a lasting impression. In addition to clear premises and conclusions, it is also important to consider the overall structure of an argument. A well-organized argument will have a logical flow, with each point building upon the last. This can be achieved by using transitions and signposts to guide the audience through the different stages of the argument. For instance, phrases such as "firstly," "secondly," and "in conclusion" can be used to indicate the progression of ideas. Similarly, using phrases like "in addition," "on the other hand," and "conversely" can help to highlight contrasting viewpoints or counterarguments. By employing these techniques, individuals can demonstrate a clear and coherent thought process, making it easier for others to follow their line of reasoning.

Structuring arguments with clear premises and conclusions can also enhance the credibility of the speaker. By presenting well-supported premises, individuals show that their arguments are based on evidence and reason rather than mere opinion. This can foster trust and confidence in the speaker, as the audience perceives them as knowledgeable and reliable sources of information. Furthermore, clear conclusions help to solidify and reinforce the main argument, demonstrating that the speaker has a strong grasp of the topic. This can further enhance the speaker's credibility and increase the persuasive impact of their message. Finally, structuring arguments with clear premises and conclusions is essential for effective communication and persuasion in various contexts. Whether it is in a formal debate, a business presentation, or a casual conversation, clear premises and conclusions provide a framework for logical and convincing arguments. They allow individuals to convey complex ideas in a succinct and understandable manner, ensuring that the audience can follow the reasoning and make informed decisions. By mastering the art of structuring arguments with clear premises and conclusions, individuals can become more persuasive communicators, able to influence others ethically and achieve their desired outcomes. Structuring arguments with clear premises and conclusions is a vital aspect of persuasive communication. Clear premises provide evidence and support for the main argument, while clear conclusions summarize the key points and leave a lasting impact on the audience. By employing techniques such as logical flow, transitions, and signposts, individuals can enhance the persuasiveness of their arguments and increase their credibility as speakers. This skill is crucial for effective communication and persuasion in a variety of contexts, enabling individuals to influence others ethically and achieve their goals.

PROVIDING EVIDENCE AND STATISTICS TO SUPPORT CLAIMS

In order to effectively persuade others, it is essential to provide evidence and statistics to support claims. Evidence and statistics serve as tangible and credible proof of the validity and reliability of our arguments, increasing the chances of influencing others ethically. When presenting evidence, it is crucial to use high-quality sources that have been thoroughly researched and peer-reviewed. The use of credible sources adds credibility to our claims and helps establish trust with the audience.

Statistics, on the other hand, present numerical data that supports the claims being made. Incorporating statistics into our persuasive communications can be highly effective in appealing to the rational side of individuals. For instance, let's consider a scenario in which we are trying to convince others to adopt a healthier lifestyle. By presenting statistics about the increasing rates of obesity and related health issues, we are providing concrete evidence of the consequences of not adopting a healthier lifestyle. Studies have shown that evidence and statistics have a significant impact on the persuasive process. A research study conducted by Tormala and Petty (2002) found that individuals who were presented with strong evidence supporting a particular claim were more likely to change their attitudes in favor of that claim compared to those who were presented with weak evidence. This illustrates the power that evidence holds in influencing individuals' beliefs and attitudes towards a particular issue.

In addition to using evidence and statistics, it is important to present this information in a clear and concise manner. The information should be easily understandable and accessible to the audience. By doing so, we are increasing the likelihood that individuals will engage with the evidence and statistics presented and consider them when forming their own opinions. Complex data should be presented in a way that is easily digestible, such as using visuals like charts or graphs to illustrate patterns and trends. Providing evidence and statistics also helps to counter potential biases and assumptions that individuals may hold. When presented with factual evidence, individuals are more likely to question their preexisting beliefs and be open to considering alternative perspectives. This is particularly important in discussions surrounding controversial topics, where emotions and personal biases may cloud judgment. Using evidence and statistics adds an element of objectivity to our arguments. It demonstrates that our claims are not solely based on personal opinions or anecdotes but are grounded in factual information. This can be particularly persuasive when trying to convince individuals who may be skeptical or resistant to change. It is important to note that providing evidence and statistics alone may not guarantee persuasion. The manner in which the information is presented and framed plays a significant role in influencing others ethically. Framing refers to how information is presented in a way that influences individuals' interpretations and judgments. By framing evidence and statistics in a way that aligns with the values and beliefs of the audience, we are more likely to effectively persuade them. Using emotional appeals in conjunction with evidence and statistics can enhance persuasive communication. Emotions play a powerful role in decision-making, and by appealing to individuals' emotions, we can create a deeper connection and resonance with our message. When presenting evidence and statistics, we can incorporate personal stories or relate the information to the experiences of the audience, making the argument more relatable and engaging. Providing evidence and statistics is a crucial aspect of persuasive communication. Evidence adds credibility and trust to our claims, while statistics appeal to individuals' rationality. By using high-quality sources, presenting information clearly, and framing the evidence and statistics in an appealing manner, we can increase the chances of influencing others ethically. Incorporating emotional appeals can further enhance the persuasive power of evidence and statistics. Effective persuasion lies in the ability to provide compelling evidence and statistics that resonate with the audience, leading to informed decisions and actions.

ANTICIPATING COUNTERARGUMENTS AND ADDRESSING THEM EFFECTIVELY

Anticipating counterarguments and addressing them effectively is a crucial aspect of persuasive communication. In order to effectively persuade others, it is important to consider and address potential objections or opposing viewpoints. By doing so, individuals can demonstrate that they have thoroughly thought through their position and are open to engaging in a constructive dialogue. Anticipating counterarguments also allows individuals to preemptively address any doubts or skepticism, thereby increasing the likelihood of their message being received more positively. One key strategy in effectively anticipating and addressing counterarguments is to put oneself in the shoes of the audience or the opposing viewpoint. By considering their perspective, individuals can identify potential objections and concerns that may arise. This requires empathy and a genuine effort to understand and acknowledge the legitimacy of different viewpoints. By adopting this approach, individuals can avoid dismissing counterarguments and instead address them empathetically, thereby fostering a more productive conversation. Anticipating counterarguments requires a thorough understanding of the topic at hand. Before engaging in persuasive communication, individuals must ensure that they have a comprehensive grasp of the subject matter. This includes being aware of different perspectives and viewpoints, as well as any evidence or data that may support or contradict one's arguments. By possessing a deep understanding of the topic, individuals are better equipped to anticipate potential objections and respond to them in a well-informed manner. Addressing counterarguments effectively also involves presenting well-reasoned and evidence-based responses. When engaging in persuasive communication, individuals must be prepared to substantiate their claims with facts, data, or logical reasoning. This not only enhances the credibility of their arguments but also demonstrates a level of intellectual rigor and integrity. By presenting well-reasoned responses, individuals can effectively deflate potential counterarguments and strengthen their overall position. Acknowledging counterarguments and showing respect for opposing viewpoints is another crucial element in persuasive communication. People are more likely to be receptive to a message when they feel their concerns and objections are being heard. By acknowledging counterarguments, individuals can demonstrate that they value an open and fair exchange of ideas. This creates an environment conducive to constructive dialogue and can help foster a sense of mutual respect, even between those with differing opinions. In addition to addressing counterarguments directly, individuals can also employ preemptive strategies to anticipate and address potential objections. This involves proactively incorporating potential counterarguments into their own arguments and addressing them before they are even raised. By doing so, individuals can strengthen their persuasiveness, as this approach demonstrates intellectual honesty and an openness to different perspectives. By preemptively addressing counterarguments, individuals can effectively neutralize potential skepticism or doubt before it arises. Another key aspect of addressing counterarguments effectively is to remain calm and composed throughout the conversation. Emotional responses can be detrimental to persuasive communication, as they may alienate the audience and hinder the exchange of ideas. By maintaining a calm and composed demeanor, individuals can create a more conducive environment for dialogue and increase the likelihood of their arguments being received more positively. This requires self-control and an ability to engage in reasoned discourse even when faced with challenging counterarguments.

Finally, it is important to recognize that addressing counterarguments does not mean winning over every single person. Persuasion is a complex process that may not always yield immediate results. It is essential to be realistic and recognize that not everyone may be convinced by one's arguments. Effectively addressing counterarguments can contribute to a broader shift in perspective over time, as individuals reflect on the points raised and consider alternative viewpoints. The goal of persuasive communication should not necessarily be to convert every single person but rather to encourage critical thinking and open up possibilities for dialogue and change. Anticipating counterarguments and addressing them effectively is a vital component of persuasive communication. By considering and addressing potential objections, individuals can demonstrate empathy, intellectual rigor, and respect for diverse viewpoints. This encourages productive dialogue and increases the likelihood of one's message being received more positively. By employing strategies such as empathizing with the audience, presenting well-reasoned responses, and maintaining composure, individuals can enhance their persuasiveness and foster a climate of mutual respect. Effectively addressing counterarguments contributes to the ethical practice of persuasion and promotes constructive change in different contexts.

E.   ETHICAL CONSIDERATIONS

Ethics play a fundamental role in persuasion and effective communication in various contexts. As individuals seeking to influence others, it is crucial to consider the ethical implications of our persuasive techniques and ensure that our intentions align with moral principles. It is important to recognize the power dynamics that exist within the act of persuasion, as well as the potential for manipulation and exploitation. A key ethical consideration is the principle of autonomy, which entails respecting the rights and choices of others. While it is natural to have goals and desired outcomes in mind when attempting to persuade, it is imperative to remember that individuals have the right to make their own decisions and form their own opinions. Ethical persuasion involves presenting information in an unbiased and transparent manner, allowing individuals to make decisions based on genuine understanding and free from coercion or manipulation.

Another ethical consideration is the principle of beneficence, which involves acting in a way that promotes the well-being and best interests of others. When persuading others, it is crucial to consider the potential impact our persuasive techniques may have on their well-being. Ethical persuasion requires us to evaluate whether our influence is genuinely beneficial or if it primarily serves our own interests. This consideration necessitates an honest reflection on our intentions and a genuine concern for the welfare of those we seek to persuade. The principle of non-maleficence urges us to do no harm. When employing persuasive techniques, it is essential to ensure that our methods do not cause harm or manipulate individuals in a way that diminishes their autonomy or well-being. This consideration is particularly important when targeting vulnerable populations, such as children, the elderly, or those who may be easily swayed. By adhering to the principle of non-maleficence, we demonstrate respect for others' rights and well-being and prioritize their best interests over our persuasive goals. Closely related to non-maleficence is the ethical consideration of truthfulness. Ethical persuasion requires a commitment to honesty and transparency, avoiding the use of deceptive tactics or misinformation to sway individuals. Honesty builds trust and credibility, allowing individuals to make informed decisions based on accurate information. Deceptive practices not only undermine trust but also impede the formation of genuine understanding and compromise the integrity of the persuasive act. The ethical communicator recognizes the importance of truthfulness and prioritizes it over short-term gains or outcomes. In addition to truthfulness, a final ethical consideration is the acknowledgment of cultural and individual differences. Persuasive techniques that may be effective in one cultural context or with one individual may not hold the same sway in another. Ethical persuasion entails recognizing and respecting these differences, avoiding the imposition of our values or beliefs on others. This consideration necessitates a willingness to adapt our persuasive techniques to the specific cultural and individual circumstances, ensuring that our influence is respectful and sensitive to diverse perspectives. Ethics are paramount in the art of persuasion and effective communication. By considering the principles of autonomy, beneficence, non-maleficence, truthfulness, and cultural sensitivity, we can navigate the complex terrain of persuasion ethically. Adhering to these ethical considerations requires a genuine concern for the well-being of those we seek to persuade and a commitment to truthfulness and transparency. By prioritizing ethical principles, we can influence others in a manner that respects their autonomy, promotes their best interests, and upholds the values of honesty, fairness, and respect. As individuals seeking to influence others, our persuasive efforts should be guided by a commitment to ethical communication and a recognition of the power and responsibility that comes with the ability to persuade.

HONESTY, TRANSPARENCY, AND INTEGRITY IN PERSUASIVE COMMUNICATION

Honesty, transparency, and integrity are essential elements in persuasive communication. When engaging in persuasion, it is crucial to maintain a sense of ethical responsibility, ensuring that the information being conveyed is truthful and accurate. Honesty in persuasive communication involves avoiding deceptive tactics and providing forthright information to the audience. This includes avoiding the use of false statistics or misleading statements that can manipulate others' perception of reality. Transparency is closely linked to honesty, involving the disclosure of any relevant information that may impact the audience's decision-making process. By being transparent, persuaders allow individuals to explore the complete picture and make informed choices based on accurate and relevant data. In addition to honesty and transparency, integrity plays a significant role in persuasive communication. Persuaders with integrity demonstrate a strong moral compass by adhering to ethical principles and avoiding manipulative behaviors. They act with the ultimate goal of benefiting others rather than solely focusing on personal gain. By embodying these values, persuaders establish trust and credibility, creating an environment conducive to open communication and genuine persuasion. Persuasive communication that incorporates honesty, transparency, and integrity allows for ethical influence by respecting the autonomy of individuals and enabling them to make informed decisions.

RESPECTING THE AUTONOMY AND INDIVIDUAL RIGHTS OF OTHERS

Respecting the autonomy and individual rights of others is a crucial aspect of effective persuasion and communication. In order to ethically influence others, it is imperative to recognize and honor the autonomy of individuals, allowing them the freedom to make their own choices and decisions. Autonomy refers to the capacity for self-governance, the ability to act and think freely without external coercion or undue influence. Respecting autonomy requires acknowledging the fundamental rights of individuals, such as the right to privacy and personal freedom of expression. When attempting to persuade others, it is essential to ensure that their autonomy is upheld and not compromised or violated. One way to respect the autonomy and individual rights of others is by maintaining an open and non-judgmental attitude. When communicating with others, it is important to approach them as equal partners in the conversation, without any preconceived notions or biases. By adopting a non-judgmental stance, we create an environment where individuals feel safe and comfortable expressing their thoughts and opinions. This fosters open and honest communication, allowing for a healthy exchange of ideas and perspectives. Respecting autonomy involves actively listening to others and valuing their viewpoints. This means genuinely paying attention to what others have to say, without interrupting or imposing our own agenda. By actively listening, we demonstrate that we value the thoughts and opinions of others, and we recognize their right to be heard. This encourages individuals to engage in the conversation and allows for a more meaningful and productive exchange of ideas.

Respecting individual rights also requires recognizing and honoring an individual's personal boundaries. Each person has their own comfort levels and limits regarding the amount of information or influence they are willing to accept. It is crucial to be aware of these boundaries and to respect them. This includes being mindful of personal space, respecting an individual's desire for privacy, and not pressuring or coercing them into making decisions that they are not comfortable with. By honoring these boundaries, we show respect for the autonomy and individual rights of others, allowing them to make choices that align with their values and beliefs. It is essential to consider the potential consequences of our persuasive attempts on others' autonomy and individual rights. While we may have good intentions, it is crucial to recognize that our actions can have unintended repercussions. Persuasion should not be used to manipulate or exploit others, as doing so infringes upon their autonomy. Instead, persuasive techniques should be employed ethically, with the goal of informing and empowering individuals to make their own choices. By considering the potential impact of our persuasive efforts, we can ensure that we respect the autonomy and individual rights of others. Respecting autonomy and individual rights is not only ethical but also enhances the effectiveness of our persuasive communication. When individuals feel that their autonomy is being respected, they are more likely to be receptive to our message and engage in a meaningful exchange. On the other hand, when individuals feel that their autonomy is being threatened or violated, they may become defensive or resistant, hindering the effectiveness of our persuasive attempts. By respecting autonomy and individual rights, we create an environment that encourages collaboration and cooperation, maximizing the chances of reaching mutually beneficial outcomes.

Respecting the autonomy and individual rights of others is fundamental to ethical persuasion and effective communication. By maintaining an open and non-judgmental attitude, actively listening, respecting personal boundaries, considering potential consequences, and valuing the autonomy of individuals, we can establish a respectful and empowering environment for persuasion. Respecting autonomy not only upholds ethical standards but also enhances the effectiveness of our persuasive communication, fostering genuine engagement and facilitating mutually beneficial outcomes. Recognizing and honoring the autonomy and individual rights of others is a hallmark of ethical persuasion and effective communication.

RECOGNIZING AND AVOIDING MANIPULATION OR COERCION

One crucial aspect of effective communication and persuasion is recognizing and avoiding manipulation or coercion. Manipulation and coercion are tactics that can be employed to influence others in unethical ways, often leading to negative consequences. Recognizing when these tactics are being used is the first step in avoiding their influence and making informed decisions. Manipulation involves the deliberate use of deceptive or dishonest tactics to achieve a desired outcome. It often involves exploiting people's emotions, vulnerabilities, and cognitive biases to gain an unfair advantage. Recognizing manipulation requires a keen understanding of human psychology and the ability to discern when someone is attempting to exploit these psychological tendencies. Coercion, on the other hand, involves the use of force or threats to gain compliance from others. It can be overt, such as physical violence or intimidation, or more subtle, such as emotional manipulation or using one's position of power to exert control. Coercion undermines the autonomy and free will of individuals, leaving them with little choice but to comply with the demands of the coercer. Avoiding manipulation and coercion requires a combination of critical thinking and assertiveness. Critically assessing the information presented to us and questioning its validity is one way to guard against manipulation. By scrutinizing the sources of information and assessing the motives and potential biases of the persuader, we can better determine if their intentions align with our own best interests.

Developing assertiveness skills is also essential in avoiding manipulation and coercion. Being assertive means expressing our needs and opinions without infringing upon the rights of others. It involves setting clear boundaries and refusing to be swayed by external pressures. Building assertiveness skills enables individuals to stay true to their own values and goals, even in the face of manipulative or coercive attempts. Another way to avoid manipulation and coercion is by cultivating self-awareness. Understanding our own vulnerabilities, biases, and emotional triggers helps us recognize when we may be more susceptible to manipulation. By taking the time to reflect on our own beliefs and values, we can strengthen our ability to make informed decisions based on what truly matters to us, rather than succumbing to external pressures. It is important to foster critical thinking skills, which can serve as a powerful defense against manipulation and coercion. Critical thinking involves analyzing information objectively, considering multiple perspectives, and evaluating the evidence presented. By honing these skills, individuals can better discern truth from falsehood and make rational decisions based on sound reasoning. Recognizing and avoiding manipulation or coercion is particularly crucial in professional contexts, where the consequences of unethical persuasion can have far-reaching effects. For example, in the world of advertising, manipulative tactics are commonly employed to influence consumer behavior and drive sales. Recognizing these tactics, such as deceptive advertising or appeals to emotion, can help individuals make more informed choices instead of falling victim to manipulation.

Similarly, in the political arena, manipulation and coercion are often used to sway public opinion and gain power. Recognizing these tactics, such as fear-mongering or misleading rhetoric, can empower individuals to critically evaluate political messages and make decisions based on their own values and beliefs rather than being swayed by manipulative tactics.

Recognizing and avoiding manipulation or coercion is a crucial skill in effectively navigating persuasive communication. Understanding the tactics used in manipulation and coercion, developing critical thinking and assertiveness skills, fostering self-awareness, and cultivating ethical decision-making are all essential steps in avoiding the negative consequences of unethical persuasion. By arming ourselves with these tools, we can protect our autonomy, make informed choices, and contribute to a more ethical and transparent society. In today's diverse and interconnected world, the ability to influence others ethically has become an increasingly valuable skill. Whether it be in business negotiations, interpersonal relationships, or even social activism, the art of persuasion plays a crucial role in shaping outcomes and driving positive change. Understanding the psychology of persuasion and effective communication is essential to ensuring that our attempts to influence others are ethical and respectful.

One of the key aspects of ethical persuasion lies in acknowledging and respecting the autonomy and agency of the individuals we seek to persuade. Persuasion, at its core, involves convincing others to adopt our point of view or take a specific course of action. We must be mindful of the fact that each person has their own beliefs, values, and priorities. Any attempt at persuasion should strive to engage and address the unique perspective of the individual in question. By recognizing and valuing their autonomy, we can create a dialogue that respects their agency and allows for an open exchange of ideas. Understanding the psychology of persuasion is another crucial component of ethical influence.

Persuasion is deeply rooted in human psychology, and being aware of the psychological principles that underlie persuasive techniques can help us navigate and employ them ethically. For instance, the principle of reciprocity suggests that people are more likely to comply with a request if they feel that someone has done them a favor in the past. It is important to approach reciprocity ethically, ensuring that the favor or concession made is genuine and not manipulative. By genuinely providing value or assistance, we can build trust and establish a foundation for ethical influence. Similarly, the principle of social proof highlights the tendency of individuals to conform to the actions or beliefs of others, particularly when uncertain or in new situations. Ethical persuasion leverages this principle by presenting credible evidence and examples that demonstrate the alignment of our point of view with the beliefs and actions of others. It is crucial to ensure that the evidence provided is accurate, reliable, and representative of a broad spectrum of perspectives. By doing so, we can avoid manipulating others into conforming to an isolated or skewed viewpoint. In addition to understanding psychological principles, effective communication lies at the heart of ethical persuasion. Through clear and concise communication, we can articulate our ideas and arguments in a manner that is respectful and easily understood by others. This involves leveraging the power of language to influence emotions, establish trust, and convey complex ideas. Ethical communicators avoid using manipulative tactics, such as exaggeration or deceptive language, that seek to deceive or exploit others. Instead, they strive for transparency and authenticity, presenting their arguments in a manner that allows individuals to make informed decisions.

Effective communication requires active listening and empathy.

By genuinely listening to and understanding the concerns and perspectives of others, we can tailor our arguments to address their underlying needs and motivations. This not only demonstrates a genuine respect for the individual but also increases the chances of successfully influencing them. By showing empathy, we create a connection and foster an environment of trust and receptiveness, enabling ethical persuasion to take place.

Context plays a significant role in ethical persuasion. Different contexts may require different approaches, and what may be persuasive in one situation may not be as effective in another. Understanding the nuances of each context and adapting our persuasive techniques accordingly is essential to ensuring that our influence remains ethical. For instance, in a business negotiation, the goal may be to find a mutually beneficial solution. In this case, a collaborative approach that highlights the benefits for all parties involved would be more ethical than one that seeks to exploit or manipulate for personal gain.

Ethical persuasion is inherently bound to the ultimate goal of promoting well-being and positive outcomes. The intentions behind our persuasive efforts should always be grounded in ethical considerations that prioritize the welfare and autonomy of others. By striving for win-win solutions and considering the long-term implications of our influence, we can ensure that our persuasion is not only effective but also morally responsible.

The art of persuasion and effective communication is a powerful tool that can drive positive change and influence others ethically. By understanding the psychology of persuasion, valuing autonomy, and adopting a genuine and empathetic communication style, we can engage in ethical and respectful influence. Recognizing the importance of context and prioritizing the well-being of others allows us to navigate different situations responsibly. Ethical persuasion is about establishing a connection, fostering trust, and working towards outcomes that benefit all parties involved.

III. APPLICATION OF PERSUASION AND EFFECTIVE COMMUNICATION

In today's complex and interconnected world, the ability to effectively persuade and communicate is of utmost importance. From the boardroom to the political arena, individuals who possess these skills can shape opinions, influence decisions, and drive significant change. It is crucial to approach persuasion with an ethical mindset, as the misuse of persuasive techniques can have serious consequences. This section will explore the application of persuasion and effective communication in various contexts, shedding light on the importance of understanding the psychology behind it. One area where persuasion and effective communication play a pivotal role is marketing and advertising. In this highly competitive field, businesses aim to capture the attention of customers and convince them to purchase their products or services. Advertisers employ a range of techniques to persuade consumers, including emotional appeals, celebrity endorsements, and storytelling. By understanding the deep-rooted desires and aspirations of their target audience, advertisers can craft messages that resonate and create a sense of urgency or desire. Ethical concerns arise when advertisers resort to deceptive tactics or manipulate vulnerable individuals. It is essential for marketers to strike a balance between capturing attention and respecting consumers' autonomy. Another domain where persuasion and effective communication are crucial is politics. Political leaders often engage in persuasion to rally public support, shape public opinion, and win elections. By employing persuasive techniques such as rhetoric, storytelling, and emotional appeals, politicians can connect with voters on an emotional level and convince them to support their policies or ideologies. Political persuasion can have both positive and negative implications. While effective communication can foster democratic participation and facilitate informed decision-making, unethical persuasion tactics, such as spreading misinformation or employing fearmongering, can undermine the democratic process and manipulate public opinion. It is therefore vital for political actors to engage in ethical persuasion and communicate transparently and honestly. Persuasion and effective communication are also central to the field of education. Teachers and educators utilize persuasive techniques to engage students, facilitate learning, and inspire critical thinking. By employing storytelling, visuals, and interactive activities, educators can capture students' attention and make complex concepts more accessible. They can utilize persuasive techniques to encourage students to adopt positive behaviors and develop essential skills. It is crucial for educators to recognize the ethical implications of persuasion in education. While persuasion can be a powerful tool for motivation and engagement, it should not be used to manipulate or coerce students. Teachers should aim to foster an environment of open dialogue, where students are encouraged to question and think critically. Persuasion and effective communication play a crucial role in the field of healthcare. Healthcare professionals often need to persuade patients to adopt healthier lifestyles, undergo specific treatments, or take medication. By using clear and empathetic communication, healthcare providers can build trust and motivate patients to make positive health choices. Ethical concerns arise when persuasion is not based on accurate information or is driven by financial incentives. It is essential for healthcare professionals to provide reliable and evidence-based information, respecting patients' autonomy and ensuring informed decision-making. Persuasion and effective communication are vital in interpersonal relationships. Whether it is a romantic relationship, a friendship, or a professional partnership, the ability to clearly communicate ideas and persuade others is essential for maintaining healthy and fulfilling connections. By employing active listening, empathy, and non-verbal communication, individuals can enhance their persuasive abilities and establish meaningful connections. It is crucial for individuals to respect the autonomy and boundaries of others. Manipulative persuasion techniques, such as gaslighting or emotional blackmail, can lead to the erosion of trust and damage relationships.

The application of persuasion and effective communication is vast and reaches different domains of our lives. Whether it is in marketing, politics, education, healthcare, or interpersonal relationships, the ability to effectively persuade and communicate is essential. It is crucial to approach persuasion ethically, understanding the psychological principles behind it and recognizing the potential for misuse. By engaging in honest, transparent, and empathetic communication, individuals can influence others while respecting their autonomy and fostering positive relationships.

A. PERSUASION IN MARKETING AND ADVERTISING

Marketing and advertising are two industries heavily reliant on the art of persuasion. In these realms, the goal is not only to inform consumers about products or services but also to influence their purchasing decisions. To achieve this, marketers and advertisers employ various persuasive strategies that tap into consumers' subconscious desires and emotions. One such strategy is the use of language that subtly creates a sense of urgency or exclusivity. Phrases like "limited time offer" or "exclusive deal" create a fear of missing out, prompting consumers to take immediate action. The use of vivid imagery and storytelling is another powerful tool in persuasion. When advertisers paint a compelling picture of how a product will improve consumers' lives or solve their problems, they create an emotional connection that can sway their decisions. The use of social proof has a significant impact on consumer behavior. When consumers see that others like them have had positive experiences with a product or service, they are more likely to trust and follow suit. Testimonials, ratings, and reviews effectively harness social proof, making consumers feel confident in their choice. Another persuasive technique widely used is the principle of reciprocity. Marketers often offer free samples or trials to consumers, prompting them to reciprocate by making a purchase. This principle taps into the innate human desire to give back in return for something received. Scarcity works as a persuasive trigger in marketing and advertising. By creating a perception of limited availability or high demand, marketers

create a sense of urgency that prompts consumers to take immediate action. Scarcity taps into the basic human instinct to acquire something that is perceived as rare or hard to obtain. Persuasion in marketing and advertising is an intricate dance between understanding consumer psychology and effectively communicating the value of a product or service.

In addition to understanding the techniques employed in marketing and advertising, it is crucial to consider the ethical implications of persuasion. Effective persuasion should adhere to ethical
standards, promoting transparency, integrity, and respect for the
consumers' autonomy. Firstly, it is essential to respect consumers' autonomy by providing them with accurate and reliable information that enables them to make informed decisions. Misleading or false advertising violates this principle and undermines
the trust consumers place in the industry. Secondly, persuasion
should be based on fostering positive and mutually beneficial relationships between consumers and marketers, rather than exploiting vulnerability or taking advantage of individuals' insecurities. Advertising that preys on individuals' fears, insecurities, or
prejudices is ethically problematic as it manipulates consumers
into making decisions they might not have otherwise made. Persuaders should be mindful of the potential for unintended consequences resulting from their persuasive efforts. For instance, persuasive marketing that encourages excessive consumption or
promotes unhealthy lifestyle choices can have detrimental effects
on individuals' physical and mental health. Hence, it is essential
to consider the long-term consequences and social implications
of the persuasive strategies employed. Finally, an ethical approach to persuasion entails recognizing the power dynamics at
play in the persuasion process. Persuaders should be aware of

their influential position and strive to empower consumers rather than overpower or manipulate them. A respectful and empathetic attitude towards consumers lays the foundation for ethical persuasion. The psychology of persuasion within marketing and advertising extends beyond the techniques used and the ethical considerations involved. It also requires an understanding of the factors that influence individuals' susceptibility to persuasion. One such factor is the persuaders' credibility and trustworthiness. Consumers are more likely to be persuaded by individuals or organizations who are perceived as experts in their field or who have a history of delivering reliable information. This highlights the importance of building and maintaining credibility in marketing and advertising efforts. Individuals' attitudes, beliefs, and values shape their susceptibility to persuasion. Persuasion is most effective when it aligns with individuals' preexisting beliefs or resonates with their values. By understanding their target audience's values and beliefs, marketers and advertisers can tailor their messages to increase the likelihood of persuasion. Individuals' personal characteristics, such as their personality traits or cognitive biases, can influence their susceptibility to persuasion. For example, individuals with a high need for cognition, or a tendency to engage in deep thinking and elaboration, are likely to be less easily persuaded by superficial or emotionally driven messages. Recognizing and accounting for such individual differences enables marketers and advertisers to develop more effective persuasive strategies. Persuasion in marketing and advertising is a multifaceted process that combines psychological understanding, effective communication, and ethical considerations. Marketers and advertisers employ various strategies, including creating a sense of urgency, using vivid imagery, harnessing social proof, leveraging reciprocity and scarcity, to influence consumers' purchasing decisions. Ethical considerations should always guide persuasive efforts, promoting transparency, integrity, and respect for consumers' autonomy. Understanding individuals' susceptibility to persuasion, including factors such as persuaders' credibility, alignment with beliefs and values, and personal characteristics, is crucial for developing effective marketing and advertising campaigns. The art of persuasion involves striking a delicate balance between achieving marketing objectives and respecting consumers' autonomy and well-being.

UTILIZING PERSUASIVE TECHNIQUES TO INFLUENCE CONSUMER BEHAVIOR

One of the most effective strategies for influencing consumer behavior is through the use of persuasive techniques. Persuasion is a skill that can be honed and utilized to great effect in various contexts, including advertising, marketing, and sales. By understanding the psychology behind persuasion and employing ethical communication strategies, individuals and organizations can effectively influence consumer behavior in a positive and responsible way. One of the key elements in utilizing persuasive techniques is understanding the target audience. Every individual is motivated by different factors, and identifying these motivations is crucial in crafting persuasive messages. This can be achieved through extensive market research and analysis, which allows for a deeper understanding of the target demographics and their needs and desires. By knowing what appeals to the target audience, persuasive messages can be tailored to effectively influence their behavior. Another important aspect of persuasive techniques is establishing credibility and trust. Consumers are more likely to be influenced by individuals or organizations they perceive as trustworthy and knowledgeable. This can be accomplished by providing accurate information, using credible sources, and demonstrating expertise in the field. By establishing credibility, consumers are more likely to view the persuasive message as reliable and credible, increasing the chances of influencing their behavior. A persuasive technique commonly used in advertising and marketing is the appeal to emotion. Emotions play a significant role in decision-making processes, and by evoking specific emotions, individuals and organizations can influence consumer behavior. For example, advertisements for luxury products often target consumers' desires for status and exclusivity, effectively appealing to their emotions and influencing their purchasing decisions. By understanding the emotions that drive consumer behavior, persuasive messages can be crafted to evoke the desired response. In addition to appealing to emotions, persuasive techniques can also utilize the principle of social proof. Social proof refers to the tendency of individuals to mimic the behavior of others when uncertain or in unfamiliar situations. By utilizing social proof, individuals and organizations can influence consumer behavior by highlighting the popularity or acceptance of a product or service. Testimonials and reviews from satisfied customers are commonly used to establish social proof and increase the likelihood of influencing consumer behavior.

Another persuasive technique that can be employed is the use of scarcity. The scarcity principle states that individuals value and desire things that are perceived as rare or limited. By creating a sense of scarcity, individuals and organizations can influence consumer behavior by increasing the perceived value and desirability of a product or service. Limited-time offers, exclusive promotions, and limited edition products are examples of how scarcity can be used to influence consumer behavior. By highlighting the scarcity or limited availability of a product or service, individuals and organizations can create a sense of urgency and drive consumers to take action. Ethical communication is essential in utilizing persuasive techniques to influence consumer behavior. It is important to ensure that the messages being communicated are truthful, accurate, and transparent. Misleading or deceptive messages can lead to negative consequences, including damage to individuals' or organizations' reputation, legal ramifications, and loss of trust from consumers. By maintaining ethical standards and promoting transparency, persuasive techniques can be employed in a responsible and trustworthy manner, effectively influencing consumer behavior without compromising integrity.

Utilizing persuasive techniques is an effective strategy in influencing consumer behavior. By understanding the psychology behind persuasion, identifying the motivations of the target audience, establishing credibility and trustworthiness, appealing to emotions, utilizing social proof and scarcity, and employing ethical communication, individuals and organizations can effectively influence consumer behavior. The art of persuasion lies in the ability to effectively communicate messages that resonate with consumers, ultimately influencing their behavior in a positive and responsible manner.

MANIPULATION AND ETHICS IN MARKETING STRATEGIES

In marketing strategies, the role of manipulation and ethics is a topic of significant importance. Manipulation refers to the deliberate and strategic influence aimed at persuading individuals to act in a certain way, while ethics refers to the moral principles that guide marketing practices. Both manipulation and ethics play a crucial role in shaping marketing strategies, as they have the power to either enhance or undermine the credibility and reputation of a brand. Manipulation in marketing strategies involves various techniques that are designed to influence and persuade consumers. These techniques, such as framing, anchoring, and social proof, tap into the psychological biases and cognitive processes of individuals to create certain desires or behaviors. For example, framing involves presenting information in a way that influences how individuals perceive and interpret it. By framing a product as "all-natural" or "organic," marketers can manipulate consumers into perceiving it as healthier or more desirable. Anchoring, on the other hand, involves presenting an initial price or value to anchor consumers' perception of subsequent prices or values. By offering a high-priced product initially and then lowering it, marketers can manipulate consumers into perceiving the lowered price as a bargain. Social proof, another technique, involves using testimonials, endorsements, or popularity to manipulate consumers into believing that others approve of or use a particular product. These techniques, when used ethically, can be effective in persuading consumers to consider or purchase a product. When used unethically or misleadingly, they can exploit consumers' vulnerabilities and undermine trust in the brand.

Ethics in marketing strategies is vital for maintaining transparency, trust, and long-term relationships with consumers. Ethical marketing practices involve aligning marketing efforts with moral principles and treating consumers with fairness and respect. This includes ensuring that marketing messages are truthful, accurate, and not misleading. One way to ensure ethical marketing practices is through the use of informed consent, which involves providing consumers with all the necessary information and allowing them to make informed decisions. For example, when marketing a product with potential health risks, marketers should clearly disclose any potential side effects, risks, or limitations. Marketers should respect consumers' privacy and confidentiality by obtaining consent before collecting, using, or sharing their personal information. Marketers should avoid exploiting vulnerable populations, such as children or those with limited decision-making abilities, and should not engage in deceptive practices, such as false advertising or bait-and-switch tactics.

Balancing manipulation and ethics in marketing strategies is a delicate task that requires marketers to consider the potential impact of their actions on consumer well-being, trust, and societal values. While manipulation can be an effective tool in persuading consumers, it should be used ethically and responsibly. Marketers should strive to create a persuasive message that is based on accurate and reliable information, rather than relying on deceptive tactics. This requires marketers to critically evaluate their marketing strategies and message to ensure they align with ethical principles. For example, instead of solely focusing on manipulating consumers' emotions, marketers should aim to provide them with relevant information, value, and benefits. By doing so, marketers can build trust and credibility with consumers, leading to stronger and more sustainable relationships.

Marketers should recognize the societal impact of their marketing strategies and consider the wider ethical implications. They should strive to avoid promoting harmful products or contributing to social issues. For instance, marketing campaigns that promote unhealthy eating habits or lifestyle choices can have detrimental effects on public health. By considering the potential consequences of their actions, marketers can contribute to promoting healthier and more responsible choices.

The role of manipulation and ethics in marketing strategies is a complex and multifaceted topic. Manipulation techniques can be used to influence consumers' behavior, but they should be employed ethically and responsibly. Ethical marketing practices are essential for maintaining trust, credibility, and long-term relationships with consumers. Marketers should aim to create persuasive messages based on accurate information and respect consumers' rights and well-being. Balancing manipulation and ethics requires critical evaluation of marketing strategies and considering the wider societal impact. By doing so, marketers can contribute to ethical and effective communication, ultimately benefiting both consumers and society as a whole.

CREATING ETHICAL ADVERTISING THAT RESPECTS CONSUMER AUTONOMY

Creating ethical advertising that respects consumer autonomy is a critical aspect of effective communication. Advertising has long been a powerful tool to persuade consumers and influence their purchasing decisions. The line between ethical and unethical advertising is often blurred, with manipulative tactics employed to exploit consumer vulnerabilities. As an ethical communicator, it is essential to prioritize consumer autonomy, ensuring that advertising messages are transparent, respectful, and promote informed decision-making. One key element of ethical advertising is transparency. Consumers have the right to be fully informed about the products or services they are being persuaded to purchase. Ethical advertisers ensure that their messages are clear, honest, and avoid any misleading or deceptive information. For instance, when advertising a food product, they provide accurate nutritional information and do not exaggerate the health benefits. Transparent advertising also entails clearly disclosing any conflicts of interest or biases that may affect the credibility of the message. By being transparent, ethical advertisers empower consumers to make informed choices based on accurate information rather than manipulating them into decisions that may not align with their needs or values. Respecting consumer autonomy in advertising also means acknowledging and honoring their individual preferences and choices. Each consumer is unique, with different needs, desires, and values. Ethical advertisers recognize this diversity and avoid making assumptions or generalizations about their target audience. Instead, they tailor their messages to different segments of the population, recognizing that a one-size-fits-all approach may not be suitable. For example, an ethical advertiser promoting a beauty product recognizes that beauty standards vary across cultures and respects the autonomy of consumers by celebrating diversity rather than imposing a narrow definition of beauty. Ethical advertising respects consumers' freedom to make choices without undue influence or manipulation. Advertisers must ensure that their messages are not excessively persuasive, coercive, or manipulative. Techniques such as fear-based advertising, false scarcity, or emotional manipulation, while effective in grabbing attention, undermine consumer autonomy. For instance, an ethical advertiser promoting a security system does not exploit fear by exaggerating crime rates or creating a sense of imminent danger. Instead, they provide objective information regarding the system's features and benefits, allowing consumers to make their own rational decisions based on their individual needs. Ethical advertising fosters informed decision-making by promoting critical thinking and consumer empowerment. Instead of simply presenting a product or service, ethical advertisers provide consumers with all the necessary information to evaluate offerings critically. They encourage consumers to compare alternatives, ask questions, and conduct additional research before making a purchase. For instance, ethical advertisers often include clear instructions on how to access additional information, such as product reviews, customer testimonials, or independent research studies. By promoting consumer empowerment, ethical advertisers allow individuals to take charge of their choices, leading to more satisfying and meaningful consumer experiences.

Ethical advertisers recognize the importance of long-term customer relationships built on trust and credibility. While unethical tactics may yield short-term gains, they often damage the reputation and trustworthiness of the advertiser in the long run. Ethical advertisers, on the other hand, prioritize establishing a genuine connection with their audience based on shared values and interests. They view advertising as an opportunity to inform and educate consumers rather than solely to persuade or sell. An ethical advertiser promoting a sustainable clothing brand, for instance, educates them on the environmental impacts of the fashion industry and empowers them to make sustainable fashion choices beyond the immediate purchase. Creating ethical advertising that respects consumer autonomy is crucial in effective communication. Transparency, respect for individual preferences, avoiding undue influence and manipulation, fostering informed decision-making, and building long-term relationships are key components of ethical advertising. Ethical advertisers prioritize the empowerment and autonomy of consumers, recognizing their right to make informed choices based on accurate and transparent information. By incorporating these principles into their advertising strategies, ethical communicators can establish trust, credibility, and meaningful connections with their audience, ultimately leading to more ethical and satisfying consumer experiences.

B. PERSUASION IN POLITICAL COMMUNICATION

Political communication is one arena where persuasion plays a crucial role in driving public opinion and shaping the course of events. The importance of persuasion in political communication is underscored by the fact that politicians and political parties invest significant time and resources in crafting persuasive messages to sway voters and gain their support. In this context, understanding the psychology of persuasion and applying it effectively becomes essential for any political communicator.

One widely recognized theory that informs persuasive communication in the political sphere is the Social Judgment Theory. This theory posits that individuals have pre-existing attitudes and values which act as anchor points or reference points. According to this theory, when politicians or political campaigners attempt to persuade individuals, they must understand where individuals stand on specific issues and then tailor their message accordingly. By making use of this understanding, they can position their message within the audience's "latitude of acceptance" – the range of opinions that an individual deems as reasonable and acceptable. Political communicators who fail to recognize this aspect risk triggering what is known as the "boomerang effect," whereby attempts at persuasion may actually push individuals away from the desired position. Persuasive political communication should also take into account the principles of cognitive dissonance theory. When individuals are presented with information that contradicts their existing beliefs or attitudes, they experience a sense of discomfort or cognitive dissonance. Political communicators can capitalize on this discomfort by presenting their message in a way that highlights the inconsistencies and contradictions within the opposing view. By doing so, they can create a psychological urge for individuals to resolve this dissonance by embracing the politician's viewpoint. It is important for political communicators to strike a balance and avoid pushing individuals further into their original position due to a defensive reaction triggered by this contradiction. The use of emotions in political persuasion has been shown to be a powerful tool in influencing public opinion. Emotions have the capability to arouse strong reactions and create lasting impressions. Political communicators often employ emotional appeals to tap into the values and aspirations of the electorate. Studies have shown that positive emotions such as hope, happiness, or pride can evoke a more favorable response towards a political candidate or party. On the other hand, negative emotions such as fear, anger, or disgust can be used as a means to criticize opponents or persuade individuals to take action against certain policies. Ethical concerns arise when emotions are exploited in a manipulative manner, crossing the line into propaganda or deceitful tactics.

In the realm of political persuasion, credibility is a vital component that can make or break a message. Persuaders must establish their credibility by demonstrating expertise, trustworthiness, and likability. For political communicators, this can be achieved through a combination of factors. Firstly, they must showcase their knowledge and experience in a particular field to gain the trust of the audience. Secondly, they should embody the qualities that the audience associates with an effective leader, such as charisma and relatability. Consistency in words and actions enhances the persuader's credibility. Any perceived inconsistency can undermine the credibility of the speaker, leading to a loss of trust and a diminished impact of their persuasive message.

Finally, the role of context in political persuasion cannot be overlooked. The effectiveness of persuasive communication can vary depending on the audience, the political climate, and the medium through which the message is delivered. Political communicators should adapt their message to suit the specific context in which they are operating. They must take into account the cultural, social, and economic factors that shape the audience's worldview. The choice of medium can impact the reception of the message. For instance, social media platforms have become increasingly important in political communication, allowing for greater reach but also creating echo chambers and filter bubbles that limit exposure to diverse perspectives. Political communicators must navigate the complex landscape of modern media while remaining true to their ethical responsibility of promoting informed dialogue and collective decision-making.

Persuasion in political communication is a multifaceted process influenced by various psychological and ethical considerations. By understanding individual attitudes, capitalizing on cognitive dissonance, harnessing the power of emotions, establishing credibility, and adapting to the context, political communicators can increase their effectiveness in persuading the public. It is crucial for political communicators to approach persuasion ethically, avoiding manipulative tactics and promoting open, honest, and informed dialogue. Only through ethically sound persuasive communication can politicians foster constructive engagement, bridge divides, and collectively work towards a better political future.

POLITICAL CAMPAIGNS AND THE ART OF PERSUASIVE MESSAGING

Political campaigns are often seen as a battleground for competing ideas, but at their core, they are also a showcase of the art of persuasive messaging. Persuasion is a powerful tool used by politicians to sway public opinion and mobilize supporters. The success of a political campaign heavily relies on the ability to craft persuasive messages that resonate with the target audience. This requires a deep understanding of human psychology and effective communication techniques. Political candidates and their teams carefully analyze the needs, values, and concerns of their constituents in order to tailor their messages accordingly.

One key aspect of persuasive messaging in political campaigns is the use of emotional appeals. Human beings are deeply influenced by their emotions, and political campaigns often tap into this aspect of human psychology. By appealing to people's fears, hopes, and desires, politicians can connect with voters on a personal level. For example, a candidate might use emotionally charged language to highlight the urgency of an issue, such as climate change or healthcare. By evoking emotions like fear, anger, or empathy, they can create a strong emotional response that motivates voters to take action.

Another important component of persuasive messaging in political campaigns is the use of logical arguments and evidence. While emotions can be a powerful motivating factor, people also respond to rational arguments backed by solid evidence. Politicians often rely on facts, figures, and statistics to support their claims and convince voters of their positions. By presenting logical reasoning and evidence, candidates aim to demonstrate their credibility and expertise on the issues they are addressing. This can help build trust and confidence in the candidate's ability to effectively address the concerns of the voters.

Persuasive messaging in political campaigns often involves the use of rhetorical devices to make messages more memorable and compelling. Rhetoric is the art of using language effectively to persuade or influence audiences. From ancient Greek philosophers to modern-day politicians, rhetoric has played a crucial role in shaping public opinion. Politicians use rhetorical devices such as metaphor, repetition, and parallelism to create memorable slogans, catchphrases, and soundbites that resonate with voters. These devices help simplify complex ideas, increase message recall, and create a sense of unity and shared values among supporters. In addition to emotional appeals, logical arguments, and rhetorical devices, political campaigns also employ persuasive messaging through the use of visuals. A striking image or a well-crafted video can leave a lasting impact on viewers and reinforce the candidate's message. Visuals have the power to evoke emotions and capture attention in a way that written or spoken words alone cannot. For example, a campaign ad showcasing a candidate interacting with diverse groups of people can convey a sense of inclusivity and empathy, while a powerful photograph of a candidate speaking to a crowd can convey charisma and leadership qualities. Visual storytelling techniques can make messages more relatable and engaging, contributing to the effectiveness of a political campaign. It is important to note that persuasive messaging in political campaigns should be done ethically and responsibly. While politicians may employ various tactics to persuade voters, it is crucial that they respect the values of honesty, transparency, and integrity. The use of manipulative or deceptive techniques can erode trust and credibility, undermining the democratic process. Ethical persuasion requires politicians to present accurate information, engage in open and respectful dialogue, and listen to the concerns of all constituents. By fostering a sense of trust and authenticity, politicians can build long-lasting relationships with voters and contribute to a healthier and more inclusive democracy. Political campaigns rely on the art of persuasive messaging to sway public opinion and mobilize supporters. By understanding human psychology, politicians craft messages that appeal to emotions, present logical arguments, use rhetorical devices, and engage visuals. Ethical considerations are paramount in political persuasion. By maintaining honesty, transparency, and integrity, politicians can build trust and credibility with voters, creating a more effective and meaningful dialogue with the electorate. The art of persuasive messaging is a powerful tool in political campaigns, and when wielded ethically, it has the potential to shape the course of societies and impact the lives of countless individuals.

ETHICAL CONSIDERATIONS IN POLITICAL PERSUASION: TRUTHFULNESS AND FAIRNESS

In the realm of political persuasion, the ethical considerations of truthfulness and fairness play a crucial role in shaping the way political campaigns are conducted. Truthfulness refers to the obligation of politicians and campaigners to convey accurate information to the public, while fairness pertains to the principle of treating all individuals and opposing viewpoints with equity and respect. These considerations are vitally important as they ensure the integrity of the democratic process and maintain the trust of the electorate. The implementation of these ethical standards can often be challenged by the complex nature of political campaigns, which are characterized by competing ideologies and the quest for power. Truthfulness is an essential ethical consideration in political persuasion because it upholds the democratic ideals of an informed electorate and accountability. When politicians engage in deceptive practices, such as spreading false information, manipulating statistics, or making promises they have no intention of fulfilling, they erode the public's trust and undermine the democratic process. For instance, during elections, voters rely on accurate information to make informed decisions about which candidate or party aligns with their values and beliefs. When politicians resort to deceptive tactics, they manipulate this decision-making process, potentially leading to outcomes that do not reflect the true will of the people. The importance of truthfulness is further emphasized by the fact that misinformation and fake news have become significant issues in recent years, with the potential to influence public opinion and shape electoral outcomes. Adherence to truthfulness is of utmost importance to ensure the authenticity and integrity of political persuasion.

Fairness is another crucial ethical consideration in political persuasion, as it fosters a democratic environment where diverse viewpoints are respected and encouraged. In a democratic society, it is essential for politicians to engage in fair discourse that gives equal opportunity to all individuals and opposing ideologies. This means treating rival candidates with respect and avoiding personal attacks or character assassinations. Politicians should also strive to present a fair representation of opposing viewpoints, acknowledging the valid concerns and arguments put forth by their opponents. By doing so, they foster a healthy and constructive political climate that promotes meaningful dialogue and encourages citizens to engage with different perspectives. Fairness in political persuasion also extends to the inclusive representation of marginalized voices and groups, ensuring that their concerns are heard and taken into account. For instance, candidates and campaigners must be cognizant of the ways in which their communication may perpetuate stereotypes or further marginalize certain communities. By embracing fairness, political campaigns can contribute to a more inclusive and representative democracy. While truthfulness and fairness are integral to ethical political persuasion, their implementation can be challenging due to the inherent complexities and competing interests involved in political campaigns. The quest for power and winning elections often puts pressure on politicians to resort to unethical tactics, such as spreading misinformation or engaging in negative campaigning. The intense competition among candidates and the desire to gain a strategic advantage can lead to a departure from ethical considerations. The influence of interest groups, political parties, and media organizations can further complicate the ethical landscape of political persuasion, as they may prioritize their own agendas or the interests of their donors over truthfulness and fairness. The rapid pace of political communication in the digital age poses challenges for truthfulness, as false information can spread quickly and be difficult to debunk. The nuances and complexities of political persuasion demand continual reflection and vigilance to ensure ethical conduct in the face of these challenges. The ethical considerations of truthfulness and fairness are integral to political persuasion and play a vital role in maintaining the integrity of the democratic process. Truthfulness ensures an informed electorate and upholds accountability, while fairness promotes inclusivity and respects diverse viewpoints. The implementation of these ethical standards can be challenging in the context of political campaigns, given the competing interests and complexities involved. Nevertheless, it is crucial for politicians and campaigners to continually reflect on their ethical responsibilities and strive to uphold truthfulness and fairness in their communication. By doing so, they contribute to the ethical practice of political persuasion and foster a democratic environment that values informed decision-making and respectful discourse.

ENSURING INFORMED DECISION-MAKING THROUGH UNBIASED DISSEMINATION OF INFORMATION

Ensuring informed decision-making through unbiased dissemination of information is a crucial aspect of ethical persuasion and effective communication. In today's fast-paced world, where information is readily available and easily accessible, it becomes essential to provide individuals with accurate and unbiased information to make informed decisions. This is particularly important in contexts such as politics, marketing, and healthcare, where persuasive tactics can often be misleading. In politics, for example, political candidates often use persuasive strategies to influence voters. These strategies may involve biased dissemination of information, leading to the manipulation of public opinion. To counteract this, it is vital to provide the public with unbiased information about different political parties, candidates, and their policies. By doing so, individuals can evaluate the information critically and make decisions based on facts, rather than being swayed by emotional appeals or false claims. Similarly, in marketing, companies often employ persuasive tactics to promote their products and services. These tactics can sometimes mislead consumers by exaggerating the benefits or downplaying the drawbacks of a particular product. To ensure informed decision-making, it is crucial for companies to provide accurate information about their products, including their features, potential risks, and customer reviews. This allows consumers to make informed choices based on their needs, preferences, and the objective information provided. Healthcare is another area where unbiased dissemination of information is of utmost importance. Patients rely on accurate and unbiased information to make decisions about their treatment options, healthcare providers, and medical procedures. In some cases, healthcare professionals may withhold or manipulate information to influence patients' decisions. This can compromise patients' autonomy and prevent them from making fully informed choices about their healthcare. To promote unbiased decision-making in healthcare, it is essential for healthcare professionals to provide patients with complete and accurate information about their diagnosis, treatment options, potential risks, and alternatives. Healthcare organizations should ensure that their communication materials, such as brochures and websites, provide unbiased information that is easily understandable for patients from diverse backgrounds. In all these contexts, unbiased dissemination of information promotes transparency, trust, and respect for individuals' autonomy. By providing individuals with accurate and objective information, they are empowered to make decisions that align with their values, preferences, and interests. Promoting unbiased dissemination of information fosters a culture of critical thinking, encouraging individuals to question misleading claims, examine evidence, and evaluate information from multiple sources. This not only benefits individuals by enhancing their ability to make informed decisions but also contributes to the overall betterment of society by ensuring that decisions are based on facts rather than manipulation or misinformation. To achieve this, effective communication plays a pivotal role. Communicators must strive to present information in a clear, concise, and unbiased manner, making it accessible to a wide range of audiences. This can be done by avoiding jargon, using understandable language, and providing supporting evidence for any claims made. Communicators should be mindful of their own biases and strive to present a balanced perspective on the topic at hand. By presenting both sides of an argument or acknowledging any limitations or counterarguments, they allow individuals to evaluate information critically and consider different viewpoints. It is important to note that unbiased dissemination of information does not mean presenting all opinions as equally valid. Rather, it involves presenting information based on evidence, facts, and reliable sources, while acknowledging differing viewpoints. Ensuring informed decision-making through unbiased dissemination of information is essential for ethical persuasion and effective communication. In contexts such as politics, marketing, and healthcare, individuals need unbiased information to make choices that align with their values, preferences, and interests. By providing accurate and objective information, communicators empower individuals to evaluate information critically, make informed decisions, and avoid manipulation or misinformation. Effective communication practices, such as using understandable language and presenting a balanced perspective, are fundamental in fostering unbiased information dissemination. Promoting unbiased communication contributes to the overall well-being of society by promoting transparency, trust, and respect for individuals' autonomy.

C. PERSUASION IN INTERPERSONAL RELATIONSHIPS

Persuasion plays a crucial role in interpersonal relationships, as it enables individuals to influence others ethically and effectively communicate their thoughts, opinions, and desires. In the context of interpersonal relationships, persuasion becomes an essential tool for achieving mutual understanding, resolving conflicts, and building trust. One effective technique of persuasion in interpersonal relationships is active listening. By attentively listening to the perspectives and concerns of others, individuals demonstrate their respect and willingness to understand the other person's viewpoint. Active listening enables individuals to gather information, identify common ground, and empathize with the emotions and experiences of others. This empathetic understanding creates a strong foundation for persuasion, as it allows individuals to tailor their messages and arguments to the specific needs and values of the person they are trying to influence. Empathy helps to establish trust and rapport, as individuals feel validated and acknowledged when their perspectives are genuinely heard. Another important aspect of persuasion in interpersonal relationships is the use of non-verbal communication. Non-verbal cues such as body language, facial expressions, and tone of voice can greatly influence the effectiveness of persuasion. Positive non-verbal cues, such as maintaining eye contact, nodding, and using open gestures, signal to the other person that their ideas are being taken seriously and encourage them to be more open to persuasion. Conversely, negative non-verbal cues, such as cross-ing arms or avoiding eye contact, may create barriers and make the other person defensive or resistant to persuasion. Individuals must be mindful of their non-verbal communication and strive to convey warmth, openness, and respect to maximize the persuasive impact of their message. Another vital aspect of persuasion in interpersonal relationships is the establishment of credibility. People are more likely to be persuaded by those they perceive as knowledgeable, reliable, and trustworthy. Thus, individuals should cultivate their expertise in the subject matter they are try-ing to influence others about, as well as consistently demonstrate integrity and consistency in their words and actions. By building credibility, individuals increase their persuasive power and likeli-hood of influencing others positively. Appealing to emotions can significantly enhance the persuasive impact of interpersonal communication. People are often swayed by emotions and per-sonal connections, so framing messages in a way that evokes strong emotional responses can be highly effective in influencing others. For instance, telling personal stories or providing relatable examples that evoke empathy can engage the emotions of the person being persuaded, leading to greater persuasion success. It is crucial to ensure that emotional appeals are ethical and au-thentic, as misleading or manipulative emotional strategies can damage trust and harm relationships in the long term. Finally, to achieve successful persuasion in interpersonal relationships, it is essential to maintain a respectful and collaborative attitude. Per-suasion should never be approached as a win-lose situation, but rather as a mutual endeavor to find common ground and reach shared goals. Utilizing active communication techniques such as reflective listening and seeking input from the other person can create an atmosphere of collaboration and cooperation. Adopting a flexible and open-minded approach allows for the consideration of alternative viewpoints, which can strengthen the persuader's argument and increase the likelihood of successful persuasion. In conclusion, persuasion in interpersonal relationships is a valuable skill that enables individuals to ethically influence others by effectively communicating their thoughts, opinions, and desires. Active listening, non-verbal communication, credibility, emotional appeals, and a respectful attitude are crucial elements of successful persuasion. By employing these strategies, individuals can build understanding, resolve conflicts, and foster trust, facilitating positive and constructive relationships.

BUILDING SUCCESSFUL RELATIONSHIPS THROUGH EFFECTIVE COMMUNICATION

Building successful relationships through effective communication is a fundamental aspect of connecting with others and fostering mutual understanding. In today's fast-paced world, where technology often acts as a barrier to face-to-face interactions, the role of effective communication becomes even more crucial. Effective communication encompasses both verbal and non-verbal aspects, enabling individuals to express themselves clearly and listen attentively to others, ultimately leading to the formation of strong and meaningful relationships.

A key factor in building successful relationships through effective communication is the ability to express oneself clearly and concisely. By articulating thoughts, ideas, and emotions in a coherent manner, individuals can ensure that their intended message is received accurately. This requires conscious effort in choosing the right words, using appropriate tone and body language, and tailoring the message to the specific context and audience. When individuals communicate with clarity, it reduces the chances of misinterpretation or confusion, thus fostering trust and establishing a solid foundation for a successful relationship.

Effective communication entails active listening, which is equally crucial in building successful relationships. Active listening involves not only hearing what the other person is saying but also paying attention to their non-verbal cues, such as body language and facial expressions. When individuals actively listen, they demonstrate a genuine interest in the other person's perspective, thoughts, and feelings. This creates a sense of validation and importance, making the other person feel valued and understood. Active listening also helps in identifying and addressing any potential barriers or conflicts, ensuring that misunderstandings are resolved promptly and relationships flourish.

In addition to clarity and active listening, effective communication necessitates empathy and emotional intelligence. Empathy allows individuals to understand and share the feelings of others, while emotional intelligence enables individuals to manage and express their own emotions appropriately. Both these qualities contribute to building successful relationships by fostering understanding, compassion, and mutual respect. When individuals can empathize with others, it creates a sense of connection and trust, enhancing the quality of interpersonal relationships. Emotional intelligence enables individuals to regulate their emotions, preventing conflicts or heated exchanges that may strain relationships. By practicing empathy and emotional intelligence, individuals can navigate through complex and sensitive conversations with tact and sensitivity, thereby building and nurturing successful relationships. Effective communication involves adapting to diverse communication styles and cultural differences. In today's globalized world, where interactions occur across borders and cultures, the ability to understand and respect different communication styles is paramount. Individuals must be open to learning and adapting to the preferences and norms of others, ensuring that their message is successfully transmitted and received. This requires individuals to be sensitive to cultural nuances, such as the use of direct or indirect communication, the importance of hierarchy and formality, and the significance of non-verbal cues. By adapting to diverse communication styles, individuals can bridge cultural gaps, foster understanding, and develop successful relationships that transcend boundaries.

Building successful relationships through effective communication requires consistent effort and a willingness to invest time and energy. Relationships, whether personal or professional, are built and nurtured through regular communication and meaningful interactions. This involves engaging in conversations, seeking feedback, resolving conflicts, and staying connected with others on a regular basis. By maintaining open lines of communication and actively participating in the relationship, individuals demonstrate their commitment and dedication, creating a strong foundation for success. It is through this continued effort that individuals can overcome challenges, celebrate achievements, and cultivate long-lasting, successful relationships. Building successful relationships through effective communication is a multifaceted process that combines various elements such as clarity, active listening, empathy, emotional intelligence, cultural adaptability, and consistency. By mastering these components, individuals can connect with others on a deeper level, foster understanding and mutual respect, and establish relationships that thrive. In a world where technological advancements often hinder face-to-face interactions, the importance of effective communication in building successful relationships cannot be overstated. As the art of persuasion and effective communication continue to evolve, individuals who prioritize and invest in developing their communication skills will undoubtedly reap the benefits of strong and meaningful connections with others.

EMPATHY, ACTIVE LISTENING, AND COMPROMISE IN INTERPERSONAL PERSUASION

In interpersonal persuasion, the key elements of empathy, active listening, and compromise play vital roles in shaping successful communication and influencing others ethically. Empathy, the ability to understand and share the feelings of another person, is a fundamental aspect of effective persuasion. By empathizing with others, individuals are better equipped to connect with their audience on an emotional level, establishing a sense of trust and rapport. This connection allows for a deeper understanding of the other person's perspective, enabling the persuader to tailor their message to resonate with the values and beliefs of their audience. By acknowledging and validating their emotions, the persuader demonstrates a genuine interest in the well-being of the other person, fostering a positive and receptive environment for persuasion. Active listening is another essential component of interpersonal communication and persuasion. In order to effectively persuade others, individuals must show a genuine interest in understanding their audience's viewpoints and concerns. Active listening involves engaging in verbal and non-verbal cues, such as maintaining eye contact, nodding, and asking clarifying questions, to demonstrate attentiveness and interest. By actively listening, persuaders not only gain valuable insight into the needs and desires of the other person but also convey respect and validation for their thoughts and feelings. This practice fosters a sense of mutual respect and understanding, opening the door for effective persuasion. A willingness to compromise is crucial in interpersonal persuasion. Effective persuaders understand that persuasive conversations are not a one-way street but rather a collaborative effort to find common ground. By being open to compromise, individuals show that they value the input and opinions of the other person, furthering the sense of respect and trust established through empathy and active listening. Compromise allows for the creation of win-win solutions, where both parties feel satisfied and invested in the outcome. This collaborative approach not only strengthens the persuader's position but also enhances the quality of the relationship, making future interactions more conducive to persuasion and cooperation.

Empathy, active listening, and compromise work synergistically to create an atmosphere of understanding and collaboration in interpersonal persuasion. By empathizing, the persuader acknowledges and understands the feelings of the other person, establishing a foundation of trust and connection. Active listening builds upon this foundation, allowing the persuader to gain valuable insights into the other person's needs and concerns. This understanding enables the persuader to tailor their message in a way that resonates with the audience, increasing the likelihood of successful persuasion. Active listening demonstrates respect and validation for the other person's perspective, creating a positive environment for discussion and cooperation. By actively listening, the persuader fosters a sense of mutual understanding and respect, strengthening the relationship and enhancing the persuader's credibility. Finally, compromise solidifies the persuasive process by creating a collaborative and mutually beneficial outcome. Willingness to compromise demonstrates the persuader's genuine interest in finding a solution that addresses both parties' needs and concerns. By considering the viewpoints and suggestions of the other person, the persuader not only shows respect but also increases the chances of reaching a satisfactory agreement. Compromise fosters a sense of ownership and investment in the outcome, leading to a more lasting and meaningful persuasion. By engaging in compromise, the persuader sets a positive example of cooperation and flexibility, enhancing the persuader's credibility and influencing others ethically.

Empathy, active listening, and compromise are essential components of successful interpersonal persuasion. Through empathy, persuaders establish a sense of trust and rapport, connecting with their audience on an emotional level. Active listening allows for a deeper understanding of the other person's perspective, enabling the persuader to tailor their message to resonate with their audience's values and beliefs. Compromise promotes collaboration and the creation of win-win solutions, ensuring a mutually beneficial outcome. When employed together, these elements create an environment of understanding and cooperation, facilitating effective persuasion while maintaining ethical standards. Mastering the art of interpersonal persuasion requires the cultivation and integration of empathy, active listening, and compromise into one's communication and persuasion techniques.

THE IMPORTANCE OF ETHICAL PERSUASION IN FOSTERING TRUST AND MUTUAL RESPECT

Effective communication and persuasion are essential skills that individuals need in various aspects of their lives. Whether it be in personal relationships, professional settings, or societal interactions, the ability to ethically persuade others is crucial in fostering trust and mutual respect. Ethical persuasion involves using logical and moral arguments to influence others without resorting to manipulation or deceit. It requires an understanding of one's audience, their values, and their perspectives, and tailoring one's approach accordingly. By employing ethical persuasion, individuals can build stronger connections, create meaningful collaborations, and promote positive change.

Trust is the foundation of any successful relationship, whether it be between friends, colleagues, or even nations. Trust cannot be acquired through force or coercion; it must be earned through honest and transparent communication. Ethical persuasion plays a key role in this process by allowing individuals to present their arguments in a sincere and respectful manner. When one resorts to manipulative tactics or uses dishonest means to sway others, trust is eroded, and relationships become fragile. In contrast, ethical persuasion helps establish trust by acknowledging the agency and autonomy of others. It recognizes that individuals have the right to make their own decisions and possess their own perspectives. By valuing the opinions and choices of others, individuals can create a foundation of trust that fosters open communication and strengthens relationships.

Ethical persuasion promotes mutual respect by encouraging individuals to consider the needs, values, and beliefs of others. It emphasizes the importance of empathy and understanding, allowing individuals to connect with their audience on a deeper level. By genuinely listening to and acknowledging the concerns and viewpoints of others, ethical persuaders can build a sense of camaraderie and shared purpose. This strengthens bonds, enhances collaboration, and nurtures a climate of mutual respect. When individuals feel that their opinions are valued, they are more willing to engage in constructive dialogue and work towards shared goals. This not only strengthens relationships but also improves the overall quality of communication and decision-making processes. Ethical persuasion is not limited to personal relationships; it is equally relevant in professional settings. In the workplace, effective communication and persuasion are paramount for successful collaborations and leadership. Ethical persuaders understand the significance of integrity and credibility in their interactions with colleagues and subordinates. They recognize that trust and respect are essential for creating a harmonious and productive work environment. By fostering an atmosphere of ethical persuasion, leaders can inspire loyalty and commitment in their teams. When employees feel that their voices are heard and their opinions matter, they are more likely to be engaged, motivated, and invested in their work. This not only leads to higher productivity but also promotes a positive organizational culture built on trust and mutual respect. Ethical persuasion is vital in societal interactions, particularly in domains such as politics and advocacy. In these contexts, the stakes are often high, and the consequences of unethical persuasion can be far-reaching. The use of manipulation, deception, or coercion can lead to division and mistrust among individuals and communities. Conversely, ethical persuasion promotes dialogue, consensus-building, and positive social change. By appealing to reason, values, and shared interests, ethical persuaders can bridge gaps and overcome differences. They recognize that true progress lies in finding common ground and working towards solutions that benefit all. By employing ethical persuasion, individuals can inspire others to take action, engage in meaningful discussions, and contribute to the betterment of society. Ethical persuasion is a fundamental component of effective communication in various realms of life. By adopting an ethical approach, individuals can build trust, foster mutual respect, and create positive change. Ethical persuasion requires individuals to value and respect the agency of others, actively listen and empathize with their perspectives, and communicate in an open and transparent manner. Whether in personal relationships, professional settings, or societal interactions, ethical persuasion is the key to establishing stronger connections, enhancing collaborations, and promoting a more inclusive and harmonious society. In a world where influence and persuasion play a crucial role in our daily lives, it becomes essential to understand the art of persuasion and its ethical implications. Persuasion, when used effectively, can help individuals communicate their ideas, convince others of their point of view, and drive positive change. The power of persuasion should be wielded responsibly, considering the psychology behind it and the contextual factors involved. Effective persuasion relies on various psychological principles that tap into the human mind's natural tendencies and cognitive biases. One such principle is the principle of consistency. People have an innate desire to be consistent in their actions and beliefs, and persuasion can leverage this predisposition. By aligning their requests with individuals' existing values or commitments, persuaders can increase the likelihood of compliance. For example, a charity seeking donations might remind individuals about their commitment to helping others and emphasize how their contribution would keep that promise. This approach appeals to the principle of consistency and increases the chances of a positive response.

Another powerful psychological principle involved in persuasion is social proof. People tend to look to others for guidance on how to behave, particularly in ambiguous situations. Persuaders can utilize this phenomenon by presenting evidence of the masses supporting a particular idea or behaving in a specific manner. For instance, testimonials or endorsements from influential figures can shape individuals' opinions and prompt them to align with the persuader's viewpoint. By showcasing a consensus, the persuader capitalizes on social proof to increase the influence of their message. Reciprocity is also a key principle in persuasion. Humans have a natural inclination to repay what they receive. When someone does a favor or provides assistance, the recipient feels obliged to reciprocate. Effective persuaders can tap into this principle by offering something of value upfront, creating a sense of indebtedness. Companies often provide free trials or samples of their products, knowing that individuals are more likely to make a purchase after receiving something for free. By leveraging the power of reciprocity, persuaders can establish a positive foundation and make their subsequent requests more compelling. While understanding the psychological principles behind persuasion is important, it is equally crucial to consider the ethical implications of influencing others. Persuasion should be used responsibly and transparently, with a genuine intent to serve the best interests of the audience. Engaging in manipulative tactics or deceiving people to achieve personal gain is not only unethical but also undermines trust and damages relationships.

To wield influence ethically, persuaders must prioritize honesty, credibility, and respect for the autonomy of their audience. They should present information accurately, avoiding distortions or exaggerations that might mislead others. Being transparent about motives and potential biases helps build trust, allowing the audience to make informed decisions. Respecting individuals' autonomy means acknowledging their freedom to accept or reject a proposed idea, without exerting undue pressure or manipulation. Effective communication is crucial in persuasion. Persuaders must tailor their message to their audience, considering their values, beliefs, and cultural background. Understanding the audience's perspective enables the persuader to connect with them on a deeper level, making the message more relatable and impactful. Active listening skills play a crucial role in effective communication. By empathetically understanding and acknowledging the concerns and viewpoints of others, persuaders can establish a genuine connection and increase the likelihood of a successful outcome. The effectiveness of persuasion is highly dependent on the context in which it is applied. Different situations require distinct communication strategies. For instance, persuading individuals to adopt a healthier lifestyle might focus on appealing to their personal goals and aspirations. On the other hand, persuading a group to support a particular cause might involve highlighting how their collective action can bring about meaningful change. By understanding the contextual factors at play, persuaders can tailor their approach to maximize their impact.

The art of persuasion is a powerful tool that can be utilized to influence others ethically. By understanding the psychological principles that underpin persuasion, persuaders can tap into natural inclinations and biases to increase their chances of success. Ethical considerations should guide the use of persuasion, prioritizing honesty, transparency, and respect for autonomy. Meticulous communication and contextual awareness further enhance the persuader's efforts. By mastering the art of persuasion ethically, individuals can foster positive change and create meaningful connections with others.

IV. CONCLUSION

The art of persuasion plays a crucial role in our daily lives, whether we are aware of it or not. Understanding the psychology behind persuasion and developing effective communication skills can greatly enhance our ability to influence others ethically. Throughout this essay, we have examined the various factors that contribute to successful persuasion, such as building credibility, employing emotions, utilizing social proof, and appealing to reason. We explored how these techniques can be applied in different contexts, including personal relationships, the workplace, and public settings. By employing ethical persuasion, we can not only create mutually beneficial outcomes but also foster empathy and understanding among individuals. It is important to remember that persuasion should not be used to manipulate or deceive others, but to genuinely engage with them and present our ideas in a compelling manner. As we navigate the increasingly complex world of communication, the art of persuasion remains a valuable skill for fostering cooperation, resolving conflicts, and influencing positive change. By understanding the psychological principles that underlie persuasion, we can become more discerning consumers of information and guard against undue influence. Mastering the art of persuasion requires practice, patience, and an ongoing commitment to ethical communication. Whether we are seeking to convince a friend to try a new restaurant, advocating for a policy change at work, or inspiring a crowd with a powerful speech, the ability to persuade others ethically is a skill that can greatly impact our personal and professional lives. As students, it is critical that we embrace the art of persuasion and recognize its significance in our academic journey. The ability to effectively articulate our arguments, engage with different perspectives, and present compelling evidence is not only valuable in the classroom but also in our future careers and personal relationships. By honing our persuasion skills, we can become more influential individuals, capable of effecting positive change in the world around us. Through ethical persuasion, we can bridge divides, encourage collaboration, and foster a more inclusive society. As we reflect on the psychology of persuasion and effective communication, let us strive to be mindful of our words, actions, and intentions. By committing to ethical practices, we can develop a persuasive power that is both influential and trustworthy. The art of persuasion is a multifaceted discipline that encompasses various skills and approaches. By understanding the psychological principles that underlie persuasion and practicing ethical communication, we can become more effective influencers in our personal and professional lives. As we navigate different contexts, it is vital that we remain mindful of the impact our words can have on others and recognize the responsibility that comes with the power to persuade. By striving for empathy, understanding, and honesty, we can make meaningful connections, bridge divides, and inspire positive change. In an increasingly interconnected world, the art of persuasion remains a compelling force that can shape our relationships, communities, and society at large.

THE ART OF PERSUASION, PSYCHOLOGY BEHIND IT, AND EFFECTIVE COMMUNICATION TECHNIQUES

As we conclude our discussion on the art of persuasion, it is important to take a moment to recap the key concepts we have explored. Throughout this essay, we have delved into the psychology behind persuasion, examining the various techniques that are employed to influence others effectively. We have seen how persuasion is deeply rooted in our innate human nature to connect with others and be heard, acknowledging the powerful impact it can have on shaping opinions and behaviors. By understanding the underlying principles of persuasion, we can use this knowledge to engage in ethical and meaningful communication. One fundamental aspect of persuasion is the understanding of human psychology. The study of psychology allows us to comprehend how people think, feel, and ultimately make decisions. By tapping into this understanding, persuaders can tailor their messages to resonate with their audience, thereby increasing the chances of influencing them. One psychological concept that plays a significant role in persuasion is cognitive dissonance. This theory posits that individuals experience discomfort when faced with conflicting beliefs or attitudes. To reduce this dissonance, individuals may adjust their attitudes or behaviors to align with new information or beliefs presented to them. Persuaders can leverage this concept by highlighting inconsistencies or contradictions in one's beliefs and then offering a solution or alternative that aligns with their desired outcome.

In addition to cognitive dissonance, another psychological principle that is heavily relied upon in the art of persuasion is social proof. Humans are inherently social creatures, and we often look to others for guidance on how to behave or what decisions to make. By presenting evidence of what others believe or do, persuaders can influence individuals to align their own attitudes or behaviors with the perceived majority. This technique has been effectively employed by marketers and advertisers, who often highlight testimonials or statistics that suggest widespread adoption of a product or service. By doing so, individuals are more likely to conform to the actions of others, feeling a sense of safety and validation in their decisions.

Effective communication techniques also play a vital role in the art of persuasion. One central concept is the importance of establishing credibility and trust with the audience. People are more likely to be persuaded by individuals they perceive as knowledgeable, reliable, and trustworthy. This can be achieved through various means, such as providing evidence, citing credible sources, or showcasing expertise in the subject matter. It is essential to convey messages in a clear and concise manner. Persuaders must be mindful of the audience's level of knowledge and tailor their language and presentation accordingly. By making the message accessible and easily digestible, persuaders increase the likelihood of their audience understanding and accepting their arguments. Another crucial aspect of effective communication is the art of active listening. Persuasion is a two-way street, and it is vital to create a space for open dialogue and exchange of ideas. By actively listening to the concerns and perspectives of others, persuaders can gain valuable insights that enable them to address objections or adapt their messaging to better resonate with the audience. Active listening fosters a sense of mutual respect and understanding, which enhances the persuader's credibility and increases the likelihood of achieving the desired outcome. Ethical considerations must be at the forefront of any persuasive communication. Persuasion should not be manipulative or coercive but rather based on transparency and respect for the autonomy of others. It is essential to present accurate and honest information, ensuring that the audience is making informed decisions. Persuaders must be conscious of the potential power dynamics at play and seek to empower rather than exploit their audience. By maintaining ethical standards in persuasive communication, the persuader builds trust and credibility, which in turn strengthens the effectiveness and impact of their message.

The art of persuasion encompasses a deep understanding of psychology, effective communication techniques, and a commitment to ethical principles. By exploring the psychology behind persuasion, we can identify the various techniques and concepts that underpin its effectiveness. By employing effective communication techniques, such as establishing credibility, active listening, and clear messaging, persuaders can engage with their audience in a meaningful and impactful manner. Finally, ethical considerations ensure that persuasion remains rooted in integrity and respect, allowing for an ethical and mutually beneficial exchange of ideas. With these tools and insights, persuaders can harness the power of persuasion to influence others ethically and foster positive change in a variety of contexts.

ETHICAL CONSIDERATIONS IN PERSUASION ACROSS VARIOUS CONTEXTS

In today's diverse and interconnected world, persuasion plays a crucial role in various aspects of our lives. From intercultural communication to marketing strategies, ethical considerations are pivotal in understanding the art of persuasion and its impact on individuals and societies. The significance of ethical considerations in persuasion cannot be overlooked as they shape our interactions and influence our decision-making processes across different contexts. Firstly, ethical considerations are paramount in the realm of intercultural communication. In an increasingly globalized world, people from different cultures and backgrounds interact on a regular basis. In such situations, persuasive techniques must be employed carefully, taking into account cultural sensitivities and values. Cultural competence is crucial to develop effective persuasive strategies that respect and take into consideration the ethical norms and beliefs of diverse populations. For example, direct and assertive persuasion techniques that are commonly employed in Western cultures may be perceived as aggressive or offensive in Eastern cultures where indirect and subtle approaches are preferred. To engage in ethical persuasion in the context of intercultural communication, one must be familiar with the cultural norms and values of different groups and adapt their persuasive techniques accordingly. In addition to intercultural communication, ethical considerations are essential in the realm of marketing and advertising. Persuasion techniques used in marketing have the potential to shape consumer behavior and influence societal values. Ethical considerations in this context involve presenting truthful and accurate information about products and services, avoiding the use of manipulative tactics, and respecting consumers' autonomy in decision-making. Unethical practices such as false advertising, misleading claims, or manipulating consumers' emotions through fear or guilt not only compromise the ethical integrity of the persuasion process but also erode public trust in the marketing industry. Conversely, ethical marketing strategies that aim for transparency, provide value to consumers, and uphold their rights contribute to building trust and long-term relationships between brands and consumers.

Ethical considerations are of utmost importance in the realm of politics and public advocacy. Political persuasion often involves shaping public opinion, mobilizing support for specific policies or candidates, and influencing voter behavior. Ethical persuasion in this context requires presenting accurate information, being transparent about the motives behind persuasive efforts, and respecting individuals' autonomy in decision-making. Political propaganda and manipulation tactics that aim to deceive or exploit people's emotions or fears not only undermine democratic principles but also erode trust in the political process. Ethical political persuasion, on the other hand, respects the rights of individuals to make informed decisions based on accurate and reliable information. Ethical considerations are significant in interpersonal relationships and social interactions. Persuasion is an inherent part of human communication, and being able to ethically influence others can strengthen relationships, build cooperation, and promote positive change. Ethical persuasion in interpersonal relationships involves respecting individuals' boundaries, being empathetic, and valuing their autonomy. Attempts to manipulate or coerce others into a particular course of action not only damage relationships but also constitute a violation of ethical principles. On the other hand, ethical persuasion involves listening actively, understanding others' perspectives, and engaging in open and honest communication that promotes mutual understanding and agreement. Ethical considerations play a vital role in persuasion across various contexts. Whether it is intercultural communication, marketing and advertising, politics and public advocacy, or interpersonal relationships, ethical persuasion involves respecting individuals' values, autonomy, and rights. Cultural competence, transparency, accuracy, and empathy are just a few examples of ethical principles that shape persuasive efforts. By understanding and applying ethical considerations in persuasion, individuals can promote positive change, build trust, and create harmonious relationships in today's interconnected world.

Emphasize the need for individuals to hone their persuasive skills ethically to establish meaningful connections, influence positive outcomes, and make informed decisions.

In today's interconnected world, the ability to persuade others is an invaluable skill that can yield numerous benefits. It is crucial to emphasize the importance of honing these skills ethically to establish meaningful connections, influence positive outcomes, and make informed decisions. Ethical persuasion entails the use of principled tactics and techniques that are grounded in honesty, integrity, and respect for others. The cultivation of such abilities is essential for individuals seeking to navigate the complexities of society and engage in effective communication across various contexts.

Ethical persuasion fosters the establishment of meaningful connections between individuals by emphasizing authenticity and empathy. When individuals engage in persuasive efforts with integrity and sincerity, they are more likely to form genuine connections with others. This enables them to understand the needs and perspectives of those they interact with, creating a foundation of trust and mutual respect.

By approaching persuasion ethically, individuals can abandon manipulative tactics and instead focus on building mutually beneficial relationships that endure beyond a single interaction. These meaningful connections have the potential to transcend superficiality and create lasting partnerships, both personally and professionally. Ethical persuasion allows individuals to influence positive outcomes in an ethical and sustainable manner. By employing ethical techniques, individuals can rely on the strength of their arguments, personal credibility, and the quality of their ideas to persuade others. When persuasion is rooted in honesty and integrity, it gives people the opportunity to be persuasive while maintaining authenticity. This approach ensures that outcomes are based on merit and fairness rather than manipulation or coercion. The influence derived from ethical persuasion is more likely to result in long-term benefits and constructive change, as it is built on true understanding and genuine conviction rather than short-term gains. Ethical persuasion enables individuals to make informed decisions that are based on a comprehensive understanding of different perspectives. When persuasion is conducted ethically, it emphasizes active listening, empathy, and the consideration of differing viewpoints. By engaging in open and respectful dialogue, individuals can broaden their understanding of complex issues and make decisions that are well-informed and balanced. Ethical persuasion prompts individuals to critically evaluate their own beliefs and biases, fostering an environment in which informed decisions can be made through thoughtful analysis and reflection. This ability to make informed decisions is crucial for individuals navigating a society saturated with persuasive messages, allowing them to resist manipulation and make choices that align with their values and goals.

Ethical persuasion is essential for promoting ethical behavior within society as a whole. By emphasizing honesty, transparency, and respect, ethical persuasion sets a standard for interpersonal communication and discourse. When individuals prioritize ethical persuasion, they contribute to a culture of integrity and mutual understanding. This not only fosters personal growth and mutual respect but also promotes a healthy and productive society. Ethical persuasion can serve as a powerful tool for positive change, as it enables individuals to advocate for causes they believe in, challenge injustice, and sway public opinion in a responsible and ethical manner. The ability to persuade others ethically is a fundamental skill that individuals must cultivate to establish meaningful connections, influence positive outcomes, and make informed decisions. Ethical persuasion promotes authenticity and empathy, allowing individuals to form genuine connections with others. By employing ethical techniques, individuals can influence positive outcomes that are fair and sustainable. Ethical persuasion also enables individuals to make informed decisions by considering diverse perspectives and engaging in open and respectful dialogue. Finally, ethical persuasion contributes to the promotion of ethical behavior within society, fostering a culture of integrity and mutual understanding. By developing ethical persuasive skills, individuals can contribute to a more ethical, empathetic, and effective communication landscape.

BIBLIOGRAPHY

Division of Behavioral and Social Sciences and Education. 'How People Learn.' Brain, Mind, Experience, and School: Expanded Edition, National Research Council, National Academies Press, 8/11/2000

Michael A. Blue. 'BUILDING CREDIBILITY IN LEADERSHIP.' Principles For Secondary Leaders, Blue Michael, God's Life Publishing, 2/16/2015

Alexandrea Creer Kahn. 'Identity Safe Classrooms, Grades 6-12.' Pathways to Belonging and Learning, Becki Cohn-Vargas, Corwin Press, 8/4/2020

Sue Hunt. 'Today's Medical Assistant.' Clinical & Administrative Procedures, Kathy Bonewit-West, BS, MEd, Elsevier Health Sciences, 10/13/2015

Leonard A Stevens. 'Listening to People.' Ralph G. Nichols, Harvard Business Review, 1/1/1957

Michael H. Hoppe. 'Active Listening: Improve Your Ability to Listen and Lead, First Edition.' Center for Creative Leadership, 5/1/2018

Sumon Mal. 'Techniques of Effective Communication.' Notion Press, 9/30/2020

George Wright. 'Behavioral Decision Making.' Springer Science & Business Media, 3/11/2013

Amos Tversky. 'Choices, Values, and Frames.' Daniel Kahneman, Cambridge University Press, 9/25/2000

Daniel Kahneman. 'Thinking, Fast and Slow.' Farrar, Straus and Giroux, 10/25/2011

David Provan. 'A Field Guide to Safety Professional Practice.' Safety Futures, 9/15/2022

James M. Byrne. 'Handbook on Crime and Technology.' Don Hummer, Edward Elgar Publishing, 3/2/2023

Murat Durmus. 'COGNITIVE BIASES A Brief Overview of Over 160 Cognitive Biases.' + Bonus Chapter: Algorithmic Bias, Lulu Press, Inc, 4/30/2022

Andrew J. DuBrin. 'Leadership: Research Findings, Practice, and Skills.' Cengage Learning, 4/8/2022

Patricia Rossi. 'Boundary Blurred: A Seamless Customer Experience in Virtual and Real Spaces.' Proceedings of the 2018 Academy of Marketing Science (AMS) Annual Conference, Nina Krey, Springer, 11/27/2018

Amanda Owen. 'The Power of Receiving.' A Revolutionary Approach to Giving Yourself the Life You Want and Deserve, Penguin, 12/23/2010

Jay A. Conger. 'The Necessary Art of Persuasion.' Harvard Business Review Press, 9/8/2008

Randal Marlin. 'Propaganda and the Ethics of Persuasion Second Edition.' Broadview Press, 9/30/2013

Robert B. Cialdini. 'Influence.' Science and Practice, Birkhauser Boston, 1/1/1980